MEDIEVAL BOSTON

and its

ARCHAEOLOGICAL IMPLICATIONS

GILLIAN HARDEN

ISBN   0 906295 00 9

Published by South Lincolnshire Archaeological Unit

The Railway Station, Heckington, Sleaford, Lincs.

and   King's Mill House, King's Mill Lane, Stamford, Lincs.

Printed by Mortons Printers, 97a East Road, Sleaford, Lincs.

© 1978   G. Harden

Copies available from the Unit offices (above)   Price: £1.25p (+ 20p p.p.)

Also published by the South Lincolnshire Archaeological Unit:

South Lincolnshire Archaeology: 1   available from the above offices.

Contents

List of Figures

The figures which are based on Ordnance Survey Maps are reproduced with the permission of the Controller of Her Majesty's Stationery Office, Crown copyright reserved.

List of Plates

Acknowledgements

Many people in Boston have given practical help towards the writing of this text and the collection of archaeological material from commercial excavations during the past fifteen months. I would like to thank Mr. K. Benton, Mrs. J. Biggadike and Mr. A. Champion, for the use of Pilgrim College Office and their facilities, and for moral support throughout the fellowship; Boston Borough Council's Planning Department, for information about planning and historic buildings, for copy dyeline facilities and for the production of the Interim Report in November 1976; volunteers from the archaeology evening class at Pilgrim College, for the recovery and washing of large quantities of pottery and leather from the Barditch and for the sorting of material in the Guildhall Museum, Boston; Sheldon Contracting Co. Ltd., for co-operation during work on the Barditch; Mr. A. Isaac, for storage and working space at Oldrid's; the many owners of properties who permitted entry and search for medieval features.

I would like to thank those who answered questions and discussed problems and indicated further areas of research in both archaeological and historical study: Mr. B. B. Simmons; Mr. J. Sleight; Miss R. H. Healey; Mr. P. Chowne; Mr. G. Bullivant; Prof. M. W. Barley; Mr. J. F. Bailey; Mr. N. J. Wright.

I am particularly grateful to Mr. D. R. Roffe for guidance in the study of medieval history and the relevant documents, and for the translation of certain Latin papers. I am also indebted to Mrs. D. M. Owen for drawing to my attention many references related to Boston in the medieval period.

I would also like to thank the staff of archive offices for making relevant material available; Boston Borough Council, for access to the Corporation's archives; Boston Library, for access to the special collection; British Museum; Cambridge University Library; Lincolnshire Archive Office; Public Record Office.

I am indebted to those who have read through the drafts of this report and made many useful suggestions and corrections: Mr. P. Chowne; Miss R. H. Healey; Miss C. M. Mahany; Mr. D. R. Roffe; Mr. B. B. Simmons.

Above all I would like to thank Mr. B. B. Simmons and Miss R. H. Healey for the patience shown and help given throughout the period of the Fellowship with Lincolnshire and Humberside Arts.

Gillian Harden
February 1978

This is published with the aid of grants from Boston Borough Council; Council for British Archaeology; C.B.A. Group 14; Department of the Environment; Pilgrim College Boston; Preservation Trust Boston; Society for Lincolnshire History and Archaeology.

Foreword

Lincolnshire and Humberside Arts have rendered yet another public service by instituting an archaeological research fellowship; they did so on the suggestion of the South Lincolnshire Archaeological Unit. They made a good choice in concentrating on Boston, with its important and distinctive history, all too long neglected.

The fellowship has been held by Miss Gillian Harden, a graduate of Leicester University, and her report is an excellent piece of work. It marshals the evidence, both published and unpublished, for the history of the town, and will be of interest and value not only to all who live in or care for it, but will be of especial use to archaeologists working there. When they work to a tight timetable, as they often must, they have little time to read the history of their site; yet without history they are digging in the dark.

The immediate financial prospects for archaeology are not bright, and amateurs and volunteers may be more than ever needed. Here is a stimulus for them.

Sir Francis Hill

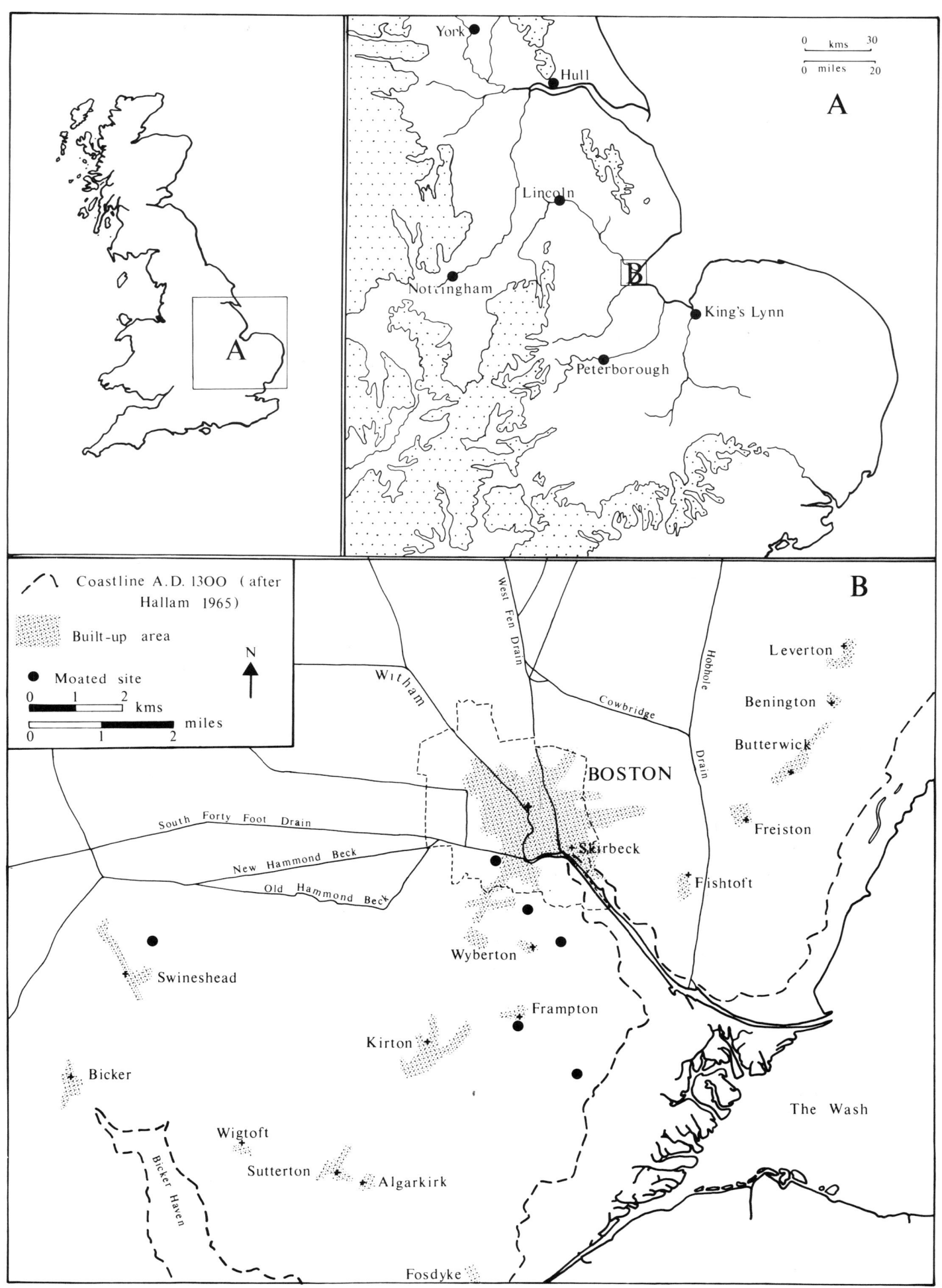

Fig. 1 *Geographical location of Boston*

1

Introduction

Scope of survey

This survey is an attempt to bring together some of the available information on Boston in the medieval period. Necessarily it includes pre-medieval and post-medieval eras, as the middle ages cannot be studied in isolation. The field of research includes historical, archaeological, topographical and architectural material, although the knowledge gleaned from these sources could and should be extended by further work. This research is not definitive: on the contrary it is aimed at encouraging others to investigate the archaeology and history of Boston, subjects sadly neglected.

Primarily it is intended that this survey should establish the need for archaeological research and excavation in the town. Archaeology can provide a detailed view of life during the phases of habitation of a site, whether it is a town, village or individual farmstead of the Prehistoric, Roman, Saxon, Medieval or Post-medieval periods. The information derived from an archaeological excavation cannot be interpreted fully, however, without knowledge being available from other disciplines. Thus, an archaeological survey should be a preliminary to any excavation, providing details of the history of a site and the problems likely to be encountered by consulting the historian, geographer, cartographer, soil scientist, botanist, chemist, et al. This can only be done successfully if the limitations and problems associated with the different subjects are understood and taken into account.

The major sources used in this survey have been historical documents, maps, topographical reproductions, extant features of the medieval townscape and archaeological finds in Boston. The problems associated with topographical research are discussed in detail on pages 16 to 18, but a general introduction to the drawbacks encountered when using historical documents is necessary.

Documents of all periods were written for a definite function and have survived through the centuries for specific reasons. Thus the records are incomplete accounts of particular periods in time, reflecting only part of the total picture of life of a certain age. They generally refer to administrative matters concerning landholders — surveys of their properties and rights, the exchange of lands, rents expected and accounted for, tolls and customs and court pleas. There are very few, if any, direct references to the poorer class of inhabitant and many questions have to be left unanswered in any detail — what did the settlement look like? How many people lived in it? Who lived where and in what? There are also many historical problems to be dealt with — what was the relationship between the upper and lower classes? What effect did several lords of the manor have on the town's development? — to mention but a few.

The interpretation of documents obviously has associated problems — to what do they actually refer? How one sided is the information presented? How important are the details that have been excluded from the written record? What do the various technical terms mean? Where information is lacking for a specific period documents of a subsequent one can be used, but the details can only be regarded as comparative in a very general way. Useful parallels can be drawn from information on similar settlements but this requires a considerable amount of background study.

Unfortunately this is by no means a complete review of the historical records related to medieval Boston. There are many documents which have not been studied, due to the limited time available. These include some at the Public Record Office and those in Kent, Durham and York. Any interpretations which are tentatively made in this survey are accordingly subject to the above limitations.

Past Archaeological Work

Boston is the only major medieval port of England which has not received the attention it deserves from those bodies which support archaeological work. Grants from the Department of the Environment and its predecessors over the past twenty years have been minimal, and no income has been forthcoming from the county, district or borough councils. Archaeological work in Boston has, therefore, been of an extremely limited nature.

A comparison of the work done in a similar medieval port, Southampton, accentuates this disparity. Southampton has had much archaeological interest, funds, and labour available over the past twenty-five years. This has resulted in the publication of two volumes of historical, architectural and archaeological information (Platt 1975). Recent texts on the history of the town have also been printed (Platt 1973; et al), whereas the history of Boston is generally taken from a large volume published in 1856 (Thompson). Other medieval ports which have been studied in detail include King's Lynn and Hull, (Parker 1971; Society for Medieval Archaeology monograph no. 7, forthcoming; Victoria History of the County of York: East Riding vol. 1, *Kingston upon Hull* ed. K. J. Allison London 1969).

The paucity of academic work on medieval Boston may be one of the reasons for the failure to attract detailed archaeological work in the past. Dr. W. I. Haward called attention to this state of affairs over forty years ago: 'Boston has played so prominent a part in the history of her country's (medieval) trade that to rescue

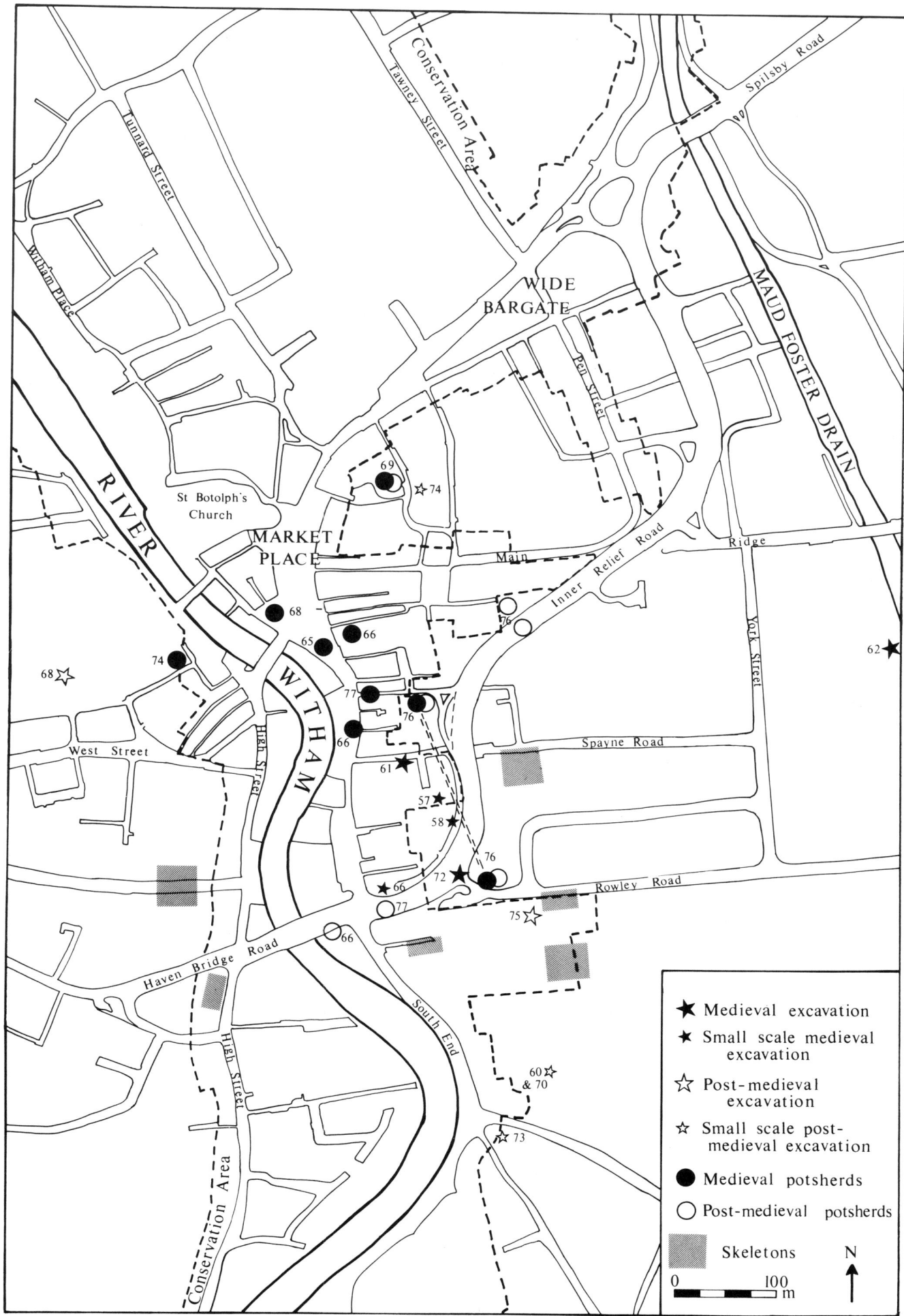

Fig. 2 *Past archaeological work in Boston*

3

that story from obscurity should be a matter of local pride, as well as of general interest.' (Haward 1933 17). Since then the destruction of archaeological sites in the town has been extensive and many buildings of historic and architectural interest have disappeared.

In the past, archaeological work has been done by local archaeologists and the Boston Archaeological Group, (which was established in 1958 after a training excavation on parts of the Barditch, directed by M. W. Barley, for Nottingham University Extra-Mural Department in 1957). The group conducted a number of minor excavations, both in and around Boston, in addition to a considerable amount of field walking and the observation of commercial excavations. The latter has resulted in the collection of medieval and post-medieval pottery, leather offcuts, wooden water pipes and the recording of human and animal bones. This work has been most useful, indicating the types of pottery that can be expected in Boston and the various periods of settlement of the town (Fig. 2). The excavations include a medieval tile kiln (Mayes 1965), exploratory trenches across the medieval boundary (information from Prof. M. W. Barley and Miss R. H. Healey), part of the Dominican Friary (excavated by Boston Archaeology Group and published by Moorhouse 1972), a post-medieval pottery kiln (information from Mr. A. J. White), and a nineteenth century clay tobacco pipe kiln (Wells 1970). These, and other excavations, are indicated on Fig. 2. Since 1970, the group's work has been severely restricted in Boston. Large scale excavations are far beyond its resources, and it has become increasingly difficult for such people to keep a constant watch on all commercial excavations that take place. Much information has, therefore, been lost; the large area of redevelopment on the west side of the Witham around Lincoln Lane is one example.

Under the system of archaeological units established by the Department of the Environment, there is now a group of professional archaeologists working in the region, the South Lincolnshire Archaeological Unit. The Department of the Environment has, however, deleted Boston from its programme, although grants have been requested for the past two years, with support from the Archaeological Area Advisory Committee. This lack of funds has limited the Unit's work in Boston. It is hoped that this situation will soon be remedied, for there is much potential labour and interest in the town, if the money and the expertise were made available.

The research that has resulted in this publication was made possible by a Fellowship from Lincolnshire and Humberside Arts' Heritage Panel. It is unusual for Regional Arts associations to support archaeological research, but they exist, in part, to preserve the heritage of the counties which they cover. The archaeology and history of Boston is an important feature of that heritage. It would be reassuring if other bodies were to follow the lead of Lincolnshire and Humberside Arts and recognise the importance of archaeology in the town's development.

Boston and District

Geographical Location

Boston is situated approximately 7km from the northwest coast of the Wash, among the fens of south Lincolnshire. The centre of the town has been built upon a varied succession of geological deposits of boulder clays, sand, peat and clays, (Wheeler 1896 App VII), now about 5m above sea level. The site is bisected by the course of the Witham which flows south-east into the Wash, (Fig. 1).

The position of this elevated area of land on both sides of the Witham provided a centre for routes of communication, both land and river, at the lowest ferry crossing of a major waterway in the middle ages.

Geological Formation

The fenland, stretching from Lincolnshire in the north to Cambridgeshire in the south, has been formed in a geological basin between the Lincolnshire Wolds and the East Anglian Heights. Glaciation affected the area, causing isostatic adjustments due to the weight of ice and, later, the deposition of great depths of boulder clays. Subsequent marine erosion and deposition have left various clays on top of these glacial deposits (Wheeler 1896 App VII 1). Thus, the area that was once a large depression became gradually silted up and islands and marshlands appeared, varying in size as the sea level changed. These alterations in the sea level have, over the past 10,000 years, caused significant changes in the coastline and associated drainage pattern of the fens.

Coastlines

Recent research into the coastline around the north and west edges of the Wash in the second century A.D., suggests that land which is today less than 3m O.D. was then below sea level (Simmons 1978). There are, of course, exceptions to this rule, but such a theory pushes the mainland coastline west by approximately 24km, with offshore islands and coastal marshes, (Fig. 3). This coastline is marked by the distribution of Roman salt-making sites along the *Midfendic*.

Although the centre of Boston is on land over 3m O.D. there are no known Roman artefacts from the town. This may indicate that the site on which Boston has developed is a comparatively recent deposit, possibly post-Roman. Alternatively it may be that any Roman remains in the town centre were buried under alluvium during the Pagan-Saxon period (see page 7).

Such changes in the coastline around the Wash imply that there must also have been variations in the natural drainage pattern of south Lincolnshire. As shown on Fig. 3, the Witham outfall during the second century A.D. was probably near Dogdyke. As the coastline moved eastwards the Witham could have had various outlets, between the existing islands, and may not have concentrated its flow in the present direction until the ninth or tenth centuries. This is a hypothetical suggestion and much research is required before it can be disproved or proved. The implication for Boston, however, would be far reaching, for it would help to explain the establishment of the settlement at Boston in the eleventh century, rather than in any preceding period.

Prehistory: before A.D. 43

Prehistoric sites and finds in and around Boston are few and far between, with the exception of a collection of flint scrapers, blades and pottery from Fishtoft. Various forms of stone axes have been recorded from Kirton, Cowbridge and Boston and bronze implements have been found in Frampton and Boston, but they were only isolated finds. Artefacts of the Iron Age have not been found in the Boston area.

Distribution maps of finds and sites of the prehistoric period in southern Lincolnshire indicate that settlement tended to be situated on the Lincolnshire Wolds, Lincoln Edge and along the Fen Edge, rather than in the fens of the county. This may be because prehistoric sites around Boston have either been buried under subsequent marine or freshwater deposits, been destroyed by the arable farmer, have yet to be discovered by the archaeologist, or did not exist. It is not yet known which of these factors is most applicable to the district around Boston, for this or the following periods.

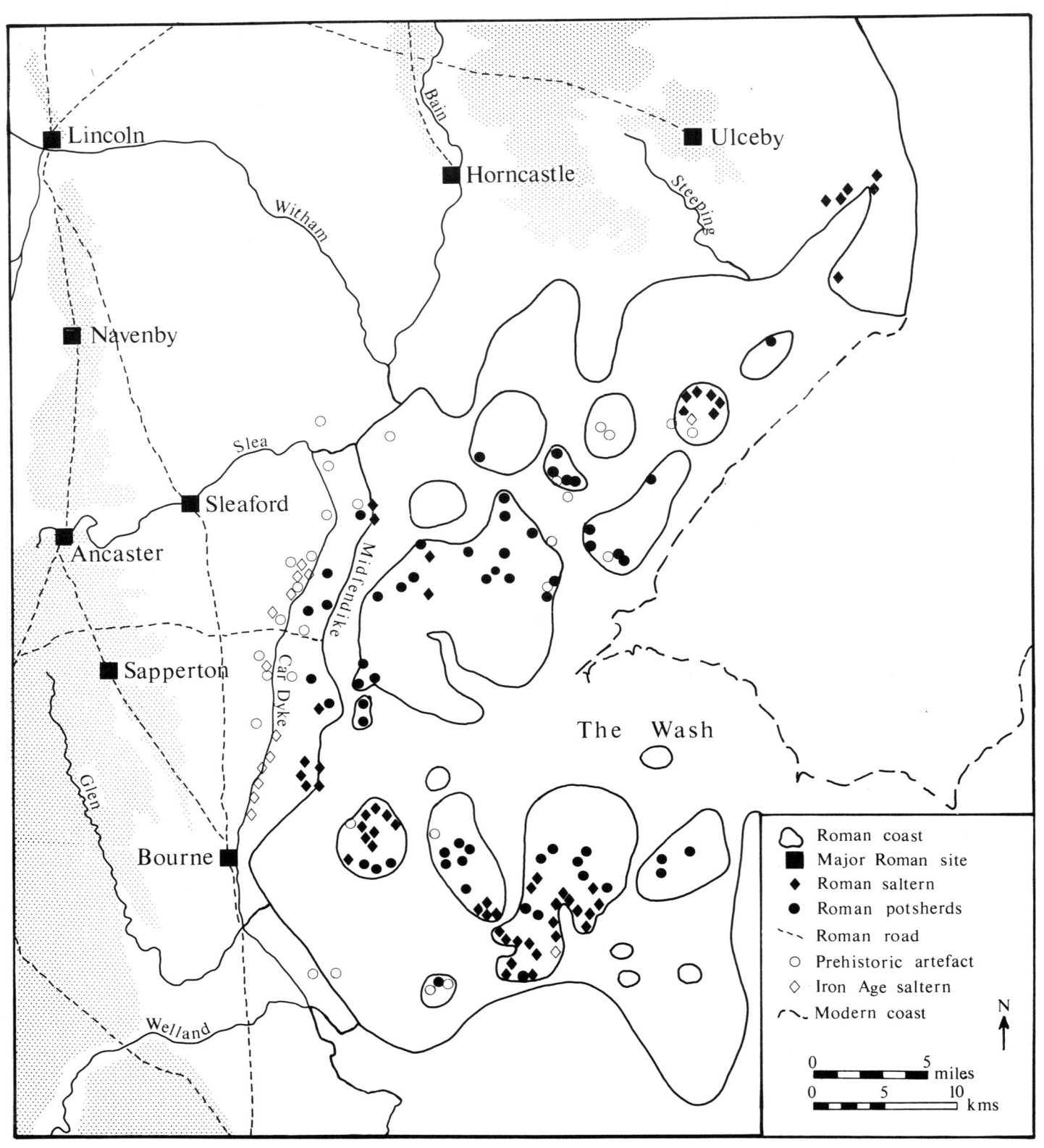

Fig. 3 *Prehistoric and Roman sites in the fens of South Lincolnshire* (by kind permission of B. B. Simmons)

Roman: A.D. 43 — A.D. 410

There is no known settlement of the Roman period in the centre of Boston. There are, however, various references to Roman remains near Boston by eighteenth and nineteenth century antiquarians. Thompson (1856 13) suggested that the earthwork to the south of Wyberton West Road had been a Roman fort at the mouth of the Witham, protecting the waterway to Lincoln. Hallam (1965 51) suggests that the earthwork is the remains of a medieval grange belonging to Stixwold Priory, a far more acceptable theory if the Witham outfall was several kilometres north-west of Boston, near Dogdyke (Fig. 3). Stukeley (1724 12) refers to a Roman milestone found on the A.16 at Wyberton, 2km south of Boston, although it may have been incorrectly identified.

There is considerable evidence of second to fourth century settlement around Boston and certain small scale excavations have taken place on parts of the sites. They include those at Boston West, Fishtoft and Wyberton Fen; with various artefacts collected from the outskirts of Boston at Woad Farm School and Skirbeck, Wyberton, Kirton End, Kirton Holme, Cowbridge and Hubberts Bridge, (Fig. 3), (information on these sites from South Lincolnshire Archaeological Unit, Lincoln Museum, Mr. J. Sleight and Mr. G. Bullivant). Major centres of Roman occupation in Lincolnshire, however, were to the west of the Car Dyke, on the Lincoln Edge and Lincolnshire Wolds, as at Horncastle, Lincoln, Sleaford and Ancaster.

Saxon: fifth century to A.D. 1000

For two hundred years after the withdrawal of the Roman administration from England there appears to have been no settlement in the region around Boston. The sea level had risen causing widespread flooding, confining Pagan-Saxon habitations to the Fen Edge.

Some of the villages near Boston, such as Frampton, Algarkirk, Burtoft and Fishtoft, were probably established during the seventh or eighth centuries A.D. Archaeological remains, place-name evidence and fragments of later Saxon architecture can be used to identify such sites, but further research is required before details of the Saxon settlement pattern in the south-east of Lincolnshire are revealed (Healey 1978).

Local mythology records that St. Botolph established his monastery at Boston in the seventh century (Thompson 1856 25-27; Cook 1948 1-2), Boston then being known as Icanho. Recent archaeological research and excavation at Hadstock, near Cambridge (Rodwell W. 1975) has led to the possible identification of the true site of Icanho. The place-name evidence for Hadstock, known as Cadenho in the middle ages, is plausible, although other sites such as Iken in Suffolk have also laid claim to this religious centre (Cook 1948 2). Boston is unlikely to be the site chosen by St. Botolph, particularly if the course of the Witham and its associated deposits in Boston were not formed until the ninth century, as suggested on page 5.

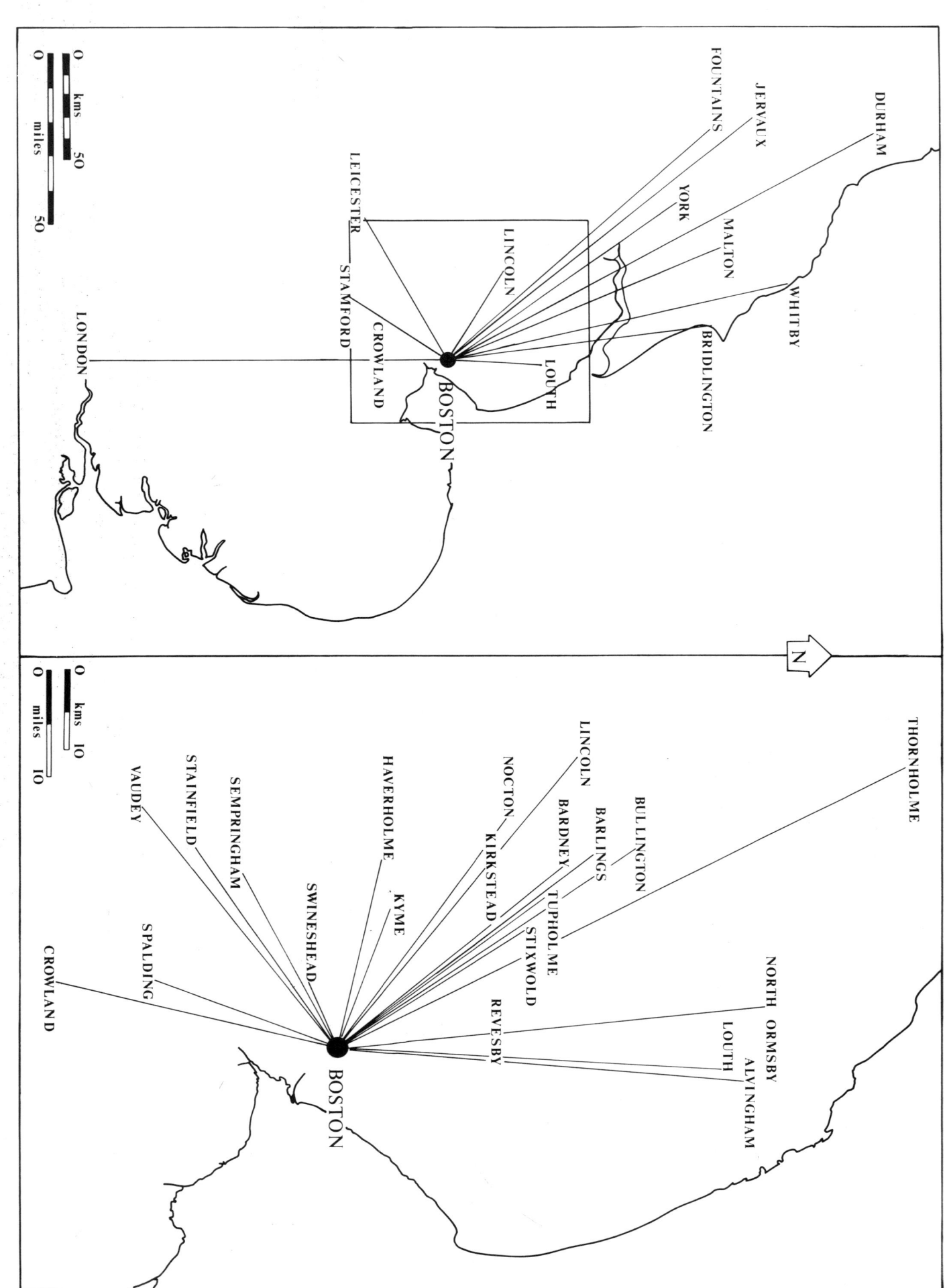

Fig. 4 *Religious houses of England with properties in Boston*

DURHAM

FOUNTAINS

JERVAUX

YORK

MALTON

WHITBY

BRIDLINGTON

LEICESTER

STAMFORD

LINCOLN

CROWLAND

BOSTON

LOUTH

LONDON

N

kms   50

miles   50

kms   50

THORNHOLME

LINCOLN

BULLINGTON

BARLINGS

NOCTON

BARDNEY

KIRKSTEAD

TUPHOLME

STIXWOLD

REVESBY

HAVERHOLME

KYME

SWINESHEAD

SEMPRINGHAM

STAINFIELD

VAUDEY

SPALDING

CROWLAND

BOSTON

NORTH ORMSBY

LOUTH

ALVINGHAM

kms   10

miles   10

kms   10

Historical Development of Boston

Boston is first mentioned in the *Registrum Antiquissimum* of Lincoln Cathedral in about A.D. 1090 (LRS 46 25), athough it is generally accepted that some form of small settlement existed at the site at the time of the Domesday Survey of 1086. The entry in the Domesday Book of lands of Count Alan, (of Richmond), in Skirbeck reads

'In Schirebec there is a berewic of Drait' (Drayton), 2 carucates of land to the geld, and in the same there is soke belonging to Drait' 9 carucates and 6 bovates of land to the geld. There is land for 8 teams. 19 sokemen and 13 villeins have 8 teams there. The count himself 1 team in demesne. There are 2 churches there, and 2 priests, and 2 fisheries rendering 10 shillings, and 40 acres of meadow.' (LRS 19 69).

In the vicinity of Skirbeck, Boston is the only settlement with a church that is not mentioned in the Domesday Book. The second church in Skirbeck, mentioned above, must therefore be Boston, particularly as St. Botolph's church was granted to St. Mary's of York by Alan, Earl of Richmond, only three years later, (BM Ad MSS 38816). There is another example of two villages in Skirbeck wapentake being treated as one in the Domesday Book, (with all the other churches in the area being accounted for), that of Butterwick and Benington (LRS 19 183).

The exclusion of certain settlements by the Domesday Survey is by no means unusual, for the assessment of geld appears to have been through the administrative centre, rather than for each individual village. Thus the Domesday Book cannot be relied upon for a complete record of the settlement pattern in southern Britain in 1086. It may instead be regarded as a reflection of the administrative organisation of regions in England in the eleventh century, or possibly earlier (Sawyer 1976 1-7).

Information on the administrative history of the town in the early thirteenth century gives an indication of the territory on which Boston was built. The two major landholders in the Boston area in 1212 were the Earl of Richmond and de Croun. The former held land in Skirbeck, Wyberton and Boston (*Book of Fees* 194-195), the latter in Wyberton (*Ibid* 194). These knights' fees can be related to those landholders mentioned in the Domesday Book. In 1086 the ancestors of de Croun held land in Wyberton (LRS 19 182) and the Earl of Richmond in Skirbeck and Wyberton (*Ibid* 69). The other landholder mentioned in the Domesday Book with land in Skirbeck is Eudo son of Spirewic (of Tatteshall) (*Ibid* 138), but there is no reference to lands of de Tatteshall in 1212. However, in 1275 (*Hundred Rolls*) de Tatteshall claimed certain rights in Boston on the west side of the Witham. There, therefore, appears to have been some continuity of landholders in the vicinity and Boston seems to have developed on lands held by them in Skirbeck and Wyberton by 1086.

Archaeological excavation may reveal evidence for the habitation of Boston in the eleventh century, but little is known of this period, for the evidence of the town's exisence is merely circumstantial.

It can be suggested that the importance of Lincoln in the early medieval period may have been fundamental to the growth of Boston. By the twelfth century Lincoln had become a major market centre for a great variety of goods, probably the most important being wool, for export as well as cloth production. Lincoln's area of trade included most of the East Midlands, and participation in foreign trade stretched from Norway to France and the Mediterranean (Hill 1948). Boston may have provided a suitable anchorage for the transfer of goods from sea-going vessels, to those able to navigate the shallow, meandering course of the Witham to Brayford Pool in Lincoln (PRO MPC 212). Thus Boston could have become involved in trade over a similar area, goods passing through the port in the twelfth and thirteenth centuries including firs, falcons, cloths and wines from northern Europe and France, and luxury items from the Mediterranean countries, such as spices, glass, silk, wax, figs and currants (Carus-Wilson 1962). Lead and iron from Derbyshire and Yorkshire were handled in Boston, as well as fish from local harbours, (*Pipe Rolls* 1175-1200).

Wool, which was probably the major export through Boston during the twelfth and thirteenth centuries, (Carus-Wilson 1963 124-140), came from religious houses and private estates in Lincolnshire, Nottinghamshire, Derbyshire and Leicestershire (*Rot. Parl* ii 332b). Although there are no known references to the use made of the properties held by religious houses in Boston (Fig. 4), it is more than likely that some were used for the storage of wool. Such buildings included those held by Louth Park (*Close Rolls* 1272-1279 321), Lincoln (*Ibid* 1288-1296 193), Fountains Abbey (*Patent Rolls* 1272-1281 141), Chester (*Ibid* 1281-1292 25) and Stanhowe (*Ibid* 122). The quantity of wool exported is not recorded in sufficient detail until the introduction of the *Ancient Custom* on wool, *woolfells*, and hides in 1275. As the late thirteenth and fourteenth centuries were a period of recession these customs accounts record the decline in the wool trade, rather than its development. Between 1275 and 1300 an average of over 8,000 sacks of wool passed through

Florence   Norway
Bordeaux   Spain
Ypres   Lombardy
Lucca   Brabant
Douai   Gascony
Toulouse   Flanders
            et al

Fig. 5 *Trade links with Boston in the thirteenth century*

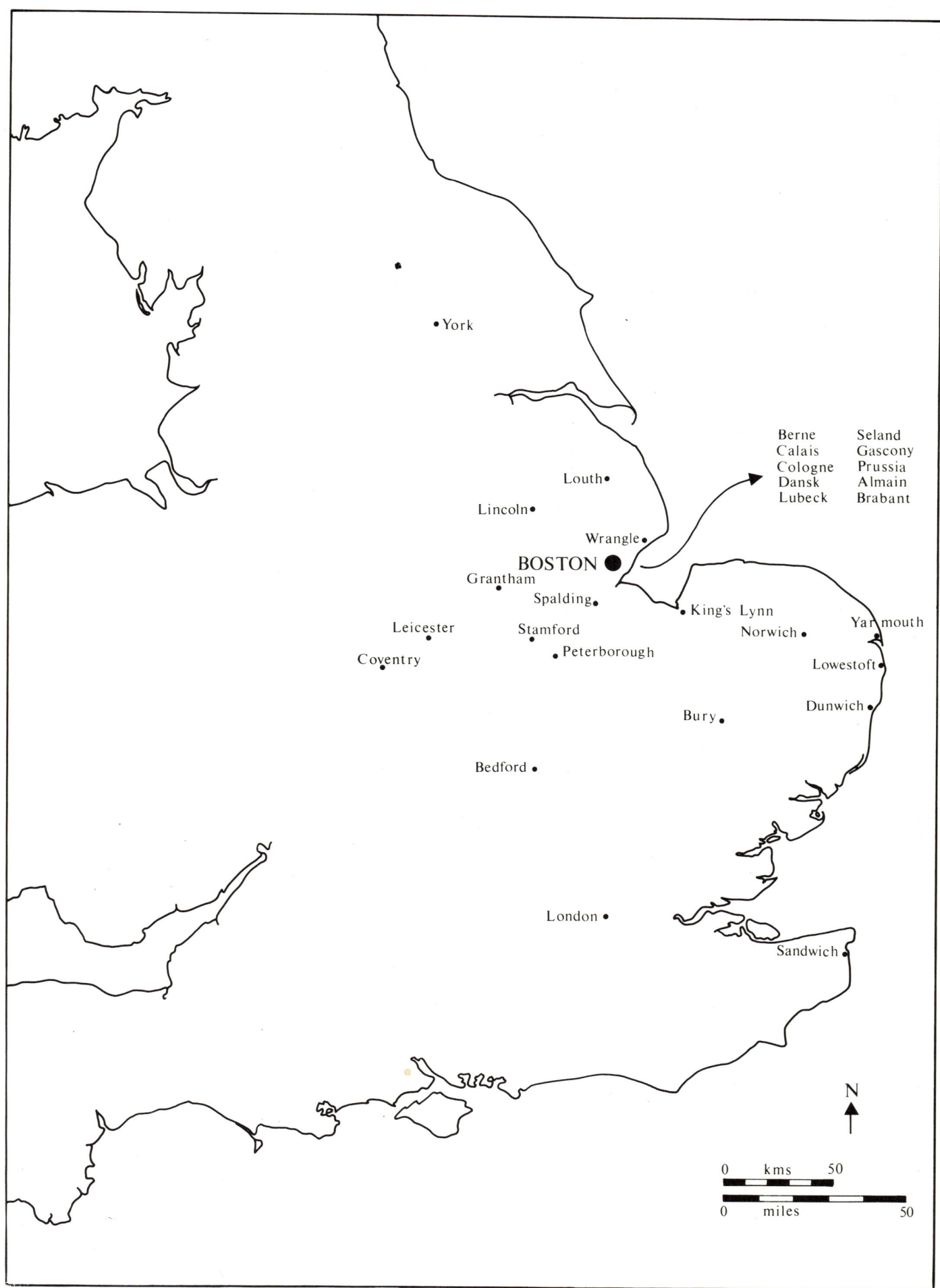

Fig. 6 Trade links with Boston in the fifteenth century

Boston each year. This compares with 7,000 sacks from London, 3,000 sacks from Hull and 3,500 sacks from Southampton during the same period, (Carus-Wilson 1963 124-140). Further research is required, but these figures are suggestive of the specialised nature of Boston's economy, possibly dependent on the export of wool. It is apparent that there was a gradual but significant change in the trade that passed through Boston during the fourteenth and fifteenth centuries. This change is most obvious in the amount of wool exported through the port. This fell from the above quantity of 8,000 sacks in 1290 to 2,500 sacks by the late fourteenth century. This presumably had a considerable effect on Boston's economy, as the port seems to have based most of its trade on wool.

During the fourteenth and fifteenth centuries the port of Boston handled a great variety of goods but these came from a smaller area than those of the previous centuries and were less in volume and regularity of delivery. Exports included hides, lead, wheat and ale (*Fine Rolls* 1337-1347 417), beans, oats, peas, rye, sheep and oxen (*Inq Misc* 3 413). Imports included herrings (*Patent Rolls* 1350-1354 390), coal from Newcastle, bricks and pantiles from the Low Countries, Spanish iron and pottery from Holland and Germany, (LRS 55 60). Luxury goods continued to be brought from the Mediterranean countries, such as in the load of *la Katerine* of Boston: wax, almonds, rice, soap, cummin, saffron, canvas, sugar, ginger, pepper, mace and vermilian, altogether worth approximately £2,000 (*Inq. Misc* 2 no. 2079).

Documents relating to the medieval period do not necessarily record the home town of merchants visiting Boston. Certain examples do exist, however, and these settlements have been mapped to give an indication of the areas of trade of Boston. The resulting maps cover complete centuries due to the lack of material for one, or even ten, continuous years. They, therefore, assume that there were no significant changes in national and international trade and economics. Such an approach has its drawbacks but it does give a general impression of Boston's sphere of influence (Figs. 5 and 6; cf Platt 1975 2 20-21). It certainly reflects a decrease in trade areas between the thirteenth and fifteenth centuries, but the flow and quantity of traffic has not been taken into account.

Boston not only served as a major entrepôt, but also as a market centre for agricultural produce and local crafts. Though there are comparatively few detailed references to this local exchange of goods from the twelfth to fifteenth centuries, archaeological material, in the form of pottery, may be indicative of the local trade area. Medieval pot sherds from the town centre of late thirteenth—early fourteenth century date have been identified as coming from kilns at Bourne (40 km), Potterhanworth (40 km), Toynton-all-Saints (25 km),

Lincoln (50 km) and Grimston (55 km). Although other medieval pottery types have been found in Boston (Fig. 7) these five major sources are from a 55 km radius around the town. This defines a rather large area for a local market centre, (Platt 1976 76) but the use of river and coastal communications in the region possibly meant that pottery and foodstuffs could easily be brought greater distances than usual. The market area for agricultural produce in the medieval period was usually the distance that could be travelled in a day on foot, within a 12 km radius (*Ibid*).

Traffic routes converged on Boston from the north, via the causeway from Stickney, from the north-west along the Witham, west and south-west by the Old Hammond Beck, along the causeways from the Fen Edge to the east and, obviously, from the North Sea and English Channel (PRO MPC 212; Thompson 1856 40).

This considerable trade through Boston and the changing nature of goods that were handled through the middle ages, imply a complex historical development of the town and port. Further research is required before details of the economic, social and cultural changes which occurred can be fully realised. The following is a synopsis of the various themes which which the future study could cover and the implications that are still to be understood.

The fair of Boston grew to be one of the most important medieval fairs in England of the thirteenth century, for it is mentioned as one of the four fairs at which the King's *prises* would be paid (*Patent Rolls* 1232-1247 239). It was well established by 1171-1172, when the first available account rendered over £60 (*Pipe Rolls* 18 *Hen II* 5). The patent for the fair, however, was not granted until 1218, when its duration was specified as the eight days following the Feast of St. John the Baptist (24 June) (*Patent Rolls* 1216-1225 157). Profits from the fair came from the court and the lease of stalls, warehouses, houses and wine cellars to merchants from England and abroad (*Pipe Roll* 2 *John* 87-89). In 1292 two cellars were leased for one week at the cost of 26s 8d, (*Inq Post Mort.* 20 *Ed* I 492) and merchants from Douai, Rouen, Caen and Cologne had houses to the east of the Witham in 1281 (*Ibid* 211). Exactly who benefitted from the profits of the fair, apart from the King, has not been explored and very useful parallels could be drawn with other fairs in the region, such as St. Ives and King's Lynn. The decline in international trade at the fair in the fourteenth century is apparent from the records relating to the difficulties of leasing land during the fair to foreign merchants (see page 29).

Although the importance of the fair diminished during the fourteenth and fifteenth centuries, the market continued to play a necessary role in the town life of Boston. The Market Place is first mentioned in the

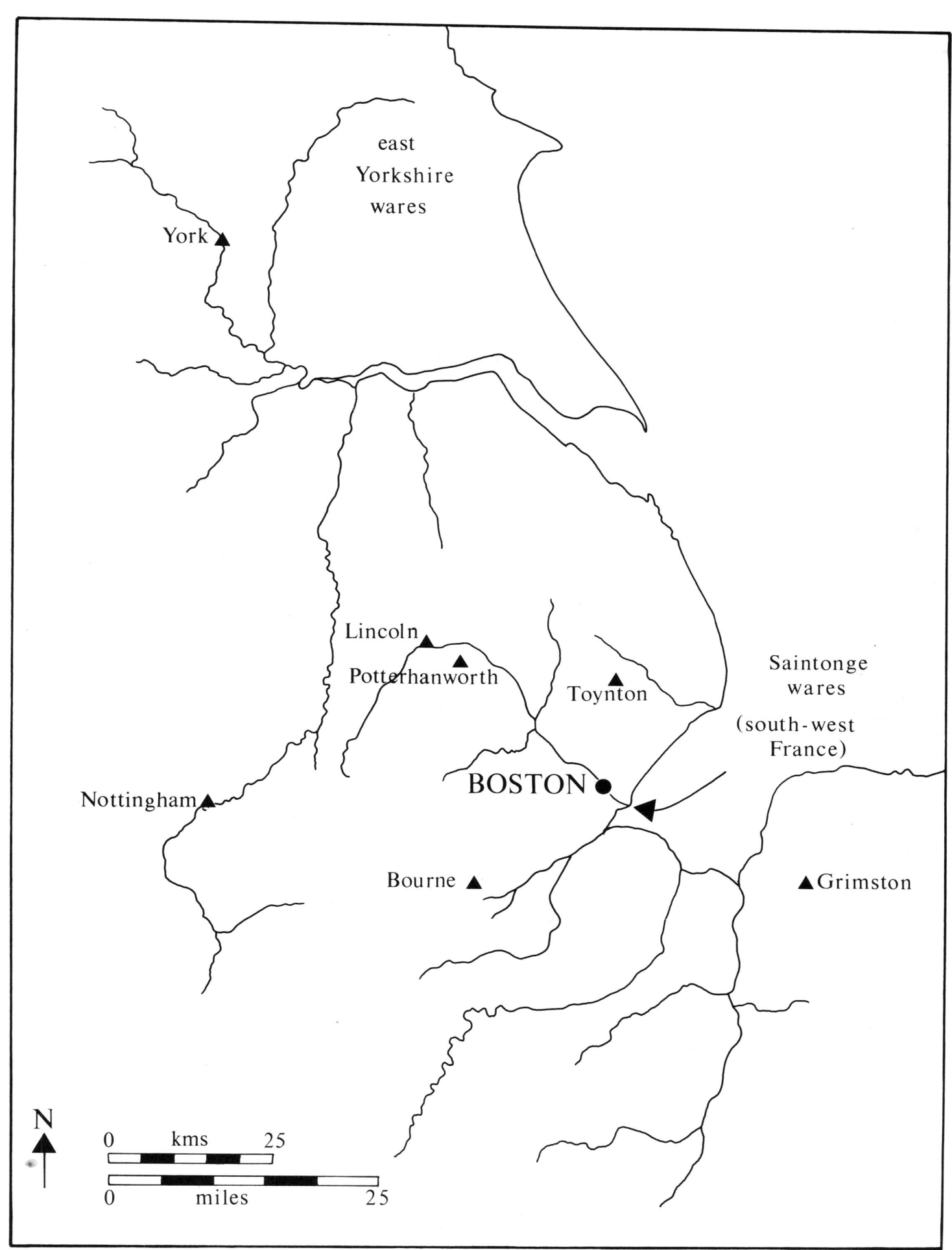

Fig. 7 *Sources of pottery imports during the thirteenth and fourteenth centuries*

late twelfth century (LRS 18 109) but the Charter for a weekly Saturday market was not granted to the Earl of Richmond until 1308 (*Charter Rolls* 1300-1326 113). It is not known whether the fair was also held in the Market Place or in Bargate (as mentioned on page 20), or whether both areas were used, but for different wares.

Boston was not incorporated until 1545 (*Letters and Papers* 1545 no. 846, 87) and, therefore, little is known of the development of the town from an element in the presumably rural estate of Skirbeck to an urban community. It is difficult not to suppose that there was some form of burgal freedom in the town by the thirteenth century, but the details and implications of this are yet to be fully understood — had the Earl of Richmond commuted certain feudal obligations so that the inhabitants of Boston were leading a comparatively free existence and did not see the need to obtain independence? or had the charter of 1204 given the men of the town the independence they required before fair and market rights had been granted? (*Pipe Roll 6 John* 76 (mentioned below).

The entrepôt and market town presumably supported a great variety of craftsmen and traders, but few are recorded in the documents of the twelfth to fifteenth centuries. Those that are mentioned in the thirteenth century include drapers and vintners (LRS 36 123) a spicer, tanner and goldsmith (LRS 51 72; LRS 46 26; LRS 22 157). The collection of archaeological material from commercial excavations can be used to expand this list to include butchers, shoe and boot makers, manufacturers of bone tools, wooden buttons and bronze buckles and rings. Archaeological excavation revealed a tile kiln outside the town centre (Mayes 1965) and future work may lead to the discovery of other local industries.

Little is known of the administration of the obviously complex historical development of Boston. The interrelationships between administration, society and topography are, however, of importance to the historian and archaeologist, particularly in deciding which site should be excavated. There are many questions relevant to these associated factors which have yet to be answered — did the rich and poor gravitate to certain different areas of the town to live? It is suggested on page 20 that Wormgate may have been an enclave of holdings of religious establishments, but whether there were similar areas in Boston elsewhere is not yet known. The names of certain lanes in the Market Place, such as *Bocher Rowe, Barborowe* and *Fysherowe,* in the fifteenth and sixteenth centuries may be indicative of specialised trades in specific parts of Boston, but archaeological excavation is required on various sites in the town before concentrations of certain ranks of society may be revealed. The rights of the native inhabitant, English merchant and foreigner living in or visiting Boston have also yet to be discovered.

The historical development of Boston is obviously associated with the changing methods of administration of the town. The complexity of the running of the town and port in the medieval period has not been studied in detail. The effects of having more than one major landholder in Boston have yet to be unravelled, for several families claimed rights and profits from the town in 1275 (*Hundred Rolls* i 348-350) — the Earl of Richmond and the families of de Croun and de Tatteshall. Their rights and control over the inhabitants of Boston are not clearly stated, but it is evident that they took rents, court profits and tolls from the fair and markets, as well as being responsible for the upkeep of the town. Both the Earl of Richmond and de Ros (of the de Croun fee) were granted *pontage* and *pavage* tolls in the early fourteenth century for the maintenance of the town bridge (*Patent Rolls*). The Earl of Richmond had his own bailiff in the town, but whether he was appointed by the Earl or elected by the inhabitants of Boston is not clear. Certainly, while the King held the Richmond fee the people of Boston were granted the right to elect their own bailiff, but it is not known if this grant continued after the fee was returned to the Richmond family (*Pipe Roll 6 John* 76).

The inhabitants of Boston had various disputes with the feudal interests of the area throughout the medieval period. Common marsh rights were contested in Wildemore Fen (*Plac. Capit. West* 79) in 1208, and the right to elect a captain and mayor of the town was temporarily grasped in 1347 (*Patent Rolls* 1345-1348 381). Other disputes were associated with the tolls which had to be paid (*Ibid* 1345-1345 298; *et al*) and assaults on individuals and their property (*Ibid* 1377-1381 421; *et al*).

The relationship between the administration of the town and port is yet another facet of Boston's development which is yet to be studied. When customs were introduced for the import and export of goods to and from England, the King had control of the port. He appointed customs collectors and controllers (*Patent Rolls*) and granted *tronage* and *pesage* rights to certain individuals, not necessarily from Boston (*Rot. Parl.* ii 213a). Once the staple was established in Boston in 1353 (*Ibid* 253a) however, the inhabitants of Boston were able to elect the mayor and constables of the staple, although those elected are not recorded in detail until the end of the fifteenth century (*Patent Rolls* 1485-1492 449).

There is obviously much research to be done before the administration of Boston can be understood and be associated with changes throughout the medieval period. That Boston appears to have undergone a significant change in the nature of the trade handled between the thirteenth and fifteenth centuries has already been mentioned (page 12). It would be foolhardy to try to identify those factors of change which were either casual or resultant, but the following are events which occurred during the late thirteenth and fourteenth centuries and which may have been associated with economic, social and cultural change.

There appears to have been a significant population decline in the late thirteenth century over most of eastern England (Bean 1962). Harvest failures resulted in famines in 1283, 1292, 1311 and, in particular, 1315-1318. Crops failed and pastures remained sodden so that feed could not be provided for sheep or cattle (Hallam 1965 123). During the early fourteenth century many private and religious estates were divided and leased, high domain farming diminished and diversification of cash crop production increased (Kershaw 1973). The centres of cloth production moved away from Lincolnshire as the profitability of the fulling mill and horizontal treddle loom were established (Carus-Wilson 1941; Miller 1965). The disruption of the production of superior cloths in Flanders went hand in hand with the decline in wool exports and the high export duty on raw wool, (Van Werveke 1954). During the middle of the fourteenth century the bubonic plague, the Hundred Years War and the restrictions on trade imposed by the King, foreign countries and the *Hansa* (James 1951; *et al*) were also contributory factors to further changes.

The removal of the staple from Lincoln to Boston in 1353 may have been an attempt to protect the trade through the port, which was already on the decline (Carus-Wilson 1963 124-140). The petition from the principal towns of the neighbouring counties that the staple should be returned to Lincoln, may, therefore, have been to protect the early medieval wool producing centres rather than a complaint that Boston had stolen their trade (*Rot. Parl.* ii 253a). It is evident, however, that the merchants of Lincoln blamed the removal of the staple to Boston for their city's economic decline by the fifteenth century, for in 1462 their poverty is quoted as a result of this change (*Patent Rolls* 1461-1467 115). The staple did not remain in Boston during the fifteenth century and other methods of protecting trade through the port may have been sought. The relationship between the staple and the establishment of gilds in the town during the late fourteenth and early fifteenth centuries is yet to be studied (*Patent Rolls* 1348-50 364; *Ibid* 1391-1396 192; *Ibid* 1399-1401 249; *et al*). The gilds that were formed in Boston were based on religious ideals, such as the gilds of Holy Trinity, St. Simon and St. Jude, and St. Katherine's (*Patent Rolls* 1408-1413 162; *Ibid* 1401-1404 388; Gibbons 1888 fo. 47). The Corpus Christi and St. Mary's gilds may have been more actively involved with trade and business, although they were also closely associated with religious beliefs. Details of the roles of the gilds in Boston are not known at present, but the latter two held extensive properties in and around Boston by the late fifteenth century (Boston Mun. Bdgs. Corpus Christi Rental; LAO Misc. Don 169).

This synopsis of the historical development of Boston is deficient in detail, but is intended to stimulate both the historian and archaeologist to study this major medieval port. Many of the problems mentioned above could be partially solved by the archaeologist in excavations, but essentially the heritage of Boston is one which can only be discovered by research in both disciplines. The archaeologist and historian are dependent on each other for information and this interdependence should be fostered. The historian, for example, can give the archaeologist information on specific areas of the town, which will affect the choice of sites to be excavated and their interpretation. Likewise, the archaeologist may provide the historian with knowledge that cannot be obtained from documents. Further research should, therefore, be undertaken in both disciplines.

Boston's Topography

Introduction

Although the methodology of creating period plans for a town is by no means straight-forward, diagrams of Boston between the thirteenth and seventeenth centuries have been produced. Before attempting to present some of the available details of the layout of Boston in the middle ages, however, it is necessary to explain the procedures of this form of research.

Knowledge of a town's topography can be derived from the present street plan, names of lanes and thoroughfares, the situation of historic buildings and property boundaries, and the concentration of archaeological material of different periods over certain areas of the urban centre. From these observations general concepts of the land covered by the medieval town can be suggested, which can be further developed by other sources of information.

In Boston these records of the past that remain today include the long narrow property boundaries, at right angles to the streets, along the east of the Market Place and the associated lanes between them. The main roads in Boston, lying parallel to the river, echoing the curves of the Witham and of a generally small width, are also medieval features. Had these roads been built in this century they would have been straight and wide, taking account of the modern form of transport. Names of various lanes and roads also suggest medieval origins, for example, Spain Lane from the de Spayne family in the fourteenth century; Emery Lane from another family of Boston in the late medieval period; and Fydell Street after the important family of that name in the eighteenth century. The situation of the various historic buildings of the town indicate both change and continuity in the layout of the street plan. The two medieval halls in High Street indicate that the line of the street frontage is little changed since the middle ages between Bridge Street and the Co-op car park. Pescod Hall in Mitre Lane, however, shows that there have been certain alterations to the length of the lane, as its medieval hall, now demolished, would have been to the west of the present building, extending over the lane. The archaeological finds from commercial excavations (Fig. 2) indicate a concentration of medieval settlement within a circumference defined by Rowley Road, Strait Bargate, Lincoln Lane and the Haven Bridge. Post-medieval material has been found over a larger area, from the south end of High Street to Hussey Tower to Wide Bargate and back across the Witham to Lincoln Lane.

Thus one has a general idea of the area of the medieval town, although there are problems. It is obvious that continual redevelopment has changed many of the property boundaries and removed a large number of historic buildings. The increasing use of heavy road transport has led to the widening and straightening of many main streets, accompanied by the addition of new roads which have to be distinguished from those of medieval origins. The names of streets or lanes may not be those of even two hundred years ago, as shown by Church Lane in Boston, called Butcher Row in 1741. Finally, the collection of archaeological material only reflects the extent of commercial excavations at which interested individuals have observed the work. It does not accurately reproduce the actual area of habitation in a period. This is even more apparent when it is considered that no Saxo-Norman potsherds have been found in Boston, although it is most likely that some form of settlement did exist late in this period.

These general observations have to be examined in greater detail if they are to be of real value to the archaeologist. The sources include maps, account and rent books of the borough and government, and various property deeds, indentures and cartularies.

Maps allow the development of a town to be traced backwards from the present day, through the very first O.S. maps of the nineteenth century, to private individuals' surveys. These were for specific purposes such as the layout of a railway, wharf or canal, enclosure award or definition of an estate. The older these maps are the less accurate they become technically, but they can provide an insight into the settlement of an area or town as far back as the seventeenth century.

For Boston, maps are available for 1972, 1887, 1829, 1811 and 1741. These have been collected together and published as *An Atlas of Boston* (Molyneux 1974). By comparing the street layout, housing and industrial premises noted on these maps, the development of the town becomes evident. The expansion of the town between 1741 and 1829 was considerable, transforming the periphery of Boston. A grid of streets was laid out between Bargate and Main Ridge and similar developments had begun north of Wormgate in Witham Green and Witham Place, and west of Rosegarth Street. The earliest map that is available for Boston is Hall's map of 1741, indicating the street plan, housing, gardens, orchards, fields and quays. Most lanes and streets are named and the more important buildings are drawn with a front elevation.

To the detailed knowledge derived from maps, information from historical documents has to be added to gain an idea of the medieval layout of the town. Similar problems are encountered in topographical research as with the study of written sources discussed on page 2. Particular difficulties occur because properties cannot be precisely located. Single accounts of the size of a messuage or tenement are given but these rarely, if ever, give details of exactly where in a street they occur.

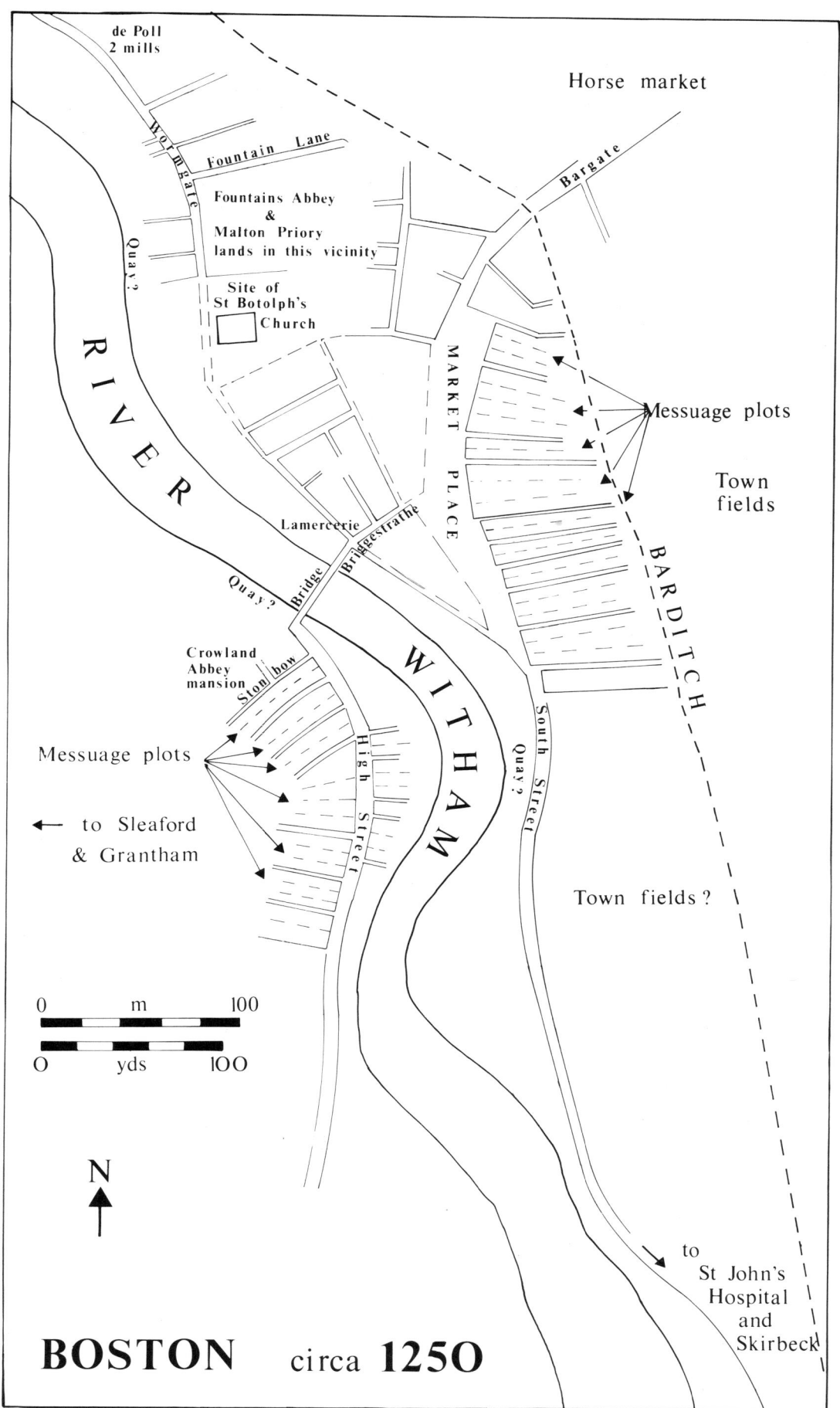

de Poll
2 mills

Horse market

Hormgate

Fountain Lane

Fountains Abbey
&
Malton Priory
lands in this vicinity

Bargate

Quay?

Site of
St Botolph's
Church

RIVER

MARKET PLACE

Messuage plots

Town
fields

Lamercerie

Briggestrathe

Quay?

Bridge

BARDITCH

Crowland
Abbey
mansion

Stonbow

WITHAM

Messuage plots

High Street

South Street

Quay?

← to Sleaford
& Grantham

Town fields ?

0   m   100

O   yds   1OO

N

to
St John's
Hospital
and
Skirbeck

BOSTON circa **1250**

Fig. 8 *A plan of Boston circa A.D. 1250*

This can be overcome when the rental gives groups of property in the same thorough-fare with one building known, or abutments, as happens in the seventeenth century Acre Books for Boston. All too often, however, a property is referred to once only and cannot be placed on a plan because not even the street or lane name is given. Other difficulties are met when the name of a house or street is not recorded on the earliest map and cannot be identified from the associated notes in the document. With these drawbacks in mind, an attempt can be made to use written records to supply information for the compilation of plans of a town in periods for which maps are not available.

In Boston, detailed accounts of the property owned by the borough in the middle of the seventeenth century are available (Boston Mun. Bdgs. Acre Books 4B/4.2; 4B/4.4). They give the tenant, rent paid, area and character of property, adjacent land and location of thoroughfares in a circuit of the town. Although such information is not comprehensive, (it does not give the precise situation of the property in a street and thus about half of the properties cannot be identified), it can be planned onto an outline of Hall's map of Boston of 1741. The plan does not give all the buildings in Boston (Fig. 10) for they were not all owned by the corporation in 1681. Neither does it accurately reflect the street layout, for one cannot assume that it was totally unchanged between 1741 and 1681. However, it does give an indication of the nature of Boston's topography in the middle of the seventeenth century.

The link with the 1741 map of Boston and the street layout of earlier centuries, becomes even more tenuous when attempts are made to plan documentary information of the medieval period. For example, there appear to be no records of building or clearance in areas such as the Market Place, although a considerable change in its open area occurred between 1741 and 1829, which may have also occurred in the past. As most of the references to specific streets or buildings occur in isolation in the medieval period, it is necessary to take information from a complete century and plan the agglomeration. Thus a plan for a whole century, rather than a point in time, such as 1887, results. It is, therefore, even more important to take into account the details of the town's topography which followed the medieval period. Documentary evidence cannot be planned in isolation but use has to be made of all the sources described above — observations, maps and post-medieval records. However, it is hoped that if the problems associated with the methods used are clearly stated then they can be criticised, and by further research the resulting plans can be improved.

The most useful accounts of the medieval period in Boston for topographical details are as follows: ministers accounts of the Richmond fee of 1435 to 1507 (PRO DL 29 and SC6), the Corpus Christi gild rental of 1489 (Boston Mun. Bdgs.), St. Mary's gild *compotus*

of 1515 (LAO Misc. Don. 169) and post-medieval records in the *Boston Corporation Minutes* of 1545 and later (Boston Mun. Bdgs.). Occasional references occur in the cartularies of the various religious houses which held property in Boston (Fig. 4), and in the Public Record Office Calendars of the *Patent Rolls, Charter Rolls* and *Close Rolls*.

The following topographical details are dealt with street by street tracing the known developments from the thirteenth to the sixteenth century. Reference should also be made to Figures 8, 9 and 10.

The Barditch

In A.D. 1200 there are the first references to the Barditch, the boundary around the east side of Boston, (LRS 46 27; LRS 18 99). Consisting of a ditch and internal bank, the earthwork was probably constructed some time during the twelfth century, but archaeological research is required before it can be dated accurately. It extended from the marsh at the north end of Wormgate (*Boston Corp. Mins.* 1558) towards what is now called St. John's Gowt, to the south of the town. The ditch presumably surrounded the twelfth century settlement, although during the thirteenth century and later, property was held outside the Barditch, indicative of urban expansion (LAO MCD 23).

These developments outside the town boundary in the middle of the thirteenth century are of particular interest. It is generally considered that mendicant orders usually built their properties on the periphery of an existing settlement (Platt 1976 37), because of the lack of space. In Boston the Dominican and Franciscan friars established their houses within the Barditch, south of the Market Place, in the second half of the thirteenth century. Expansion outside the boundary, however, was already in existence. Was this development due to the importance of a specific area as a market, such as Bargate? Or were the friaries built on lands that already had buildings on them, but which were subsequently donated to the mendicant orders? Further research is required, but from the information at present available the former is more likely. The donations to the various friaries tend to be recorded as acres of land rather than as messuages or tenements (*Patent Rolls* 1317-1321 89; *et al*), except in the case of the Carmelite Friary on the west side of the Witham (*Patent Rolls* 1301-1307 364).

Whether the Barditch was ever of a defensive nature is open to question. The bridge across the Barditch in Bargate would have provided a suitable place for the collection of tolls from those visiting the fair and markets (*Curia Regis Rolls* 1207-1209 45, 73, 136). The length of the ditch was used as an open sewer and rubbish tip, particularly by those inhabitants whose messuage plots abutted it, (*Charter Rolls* 1327-1341

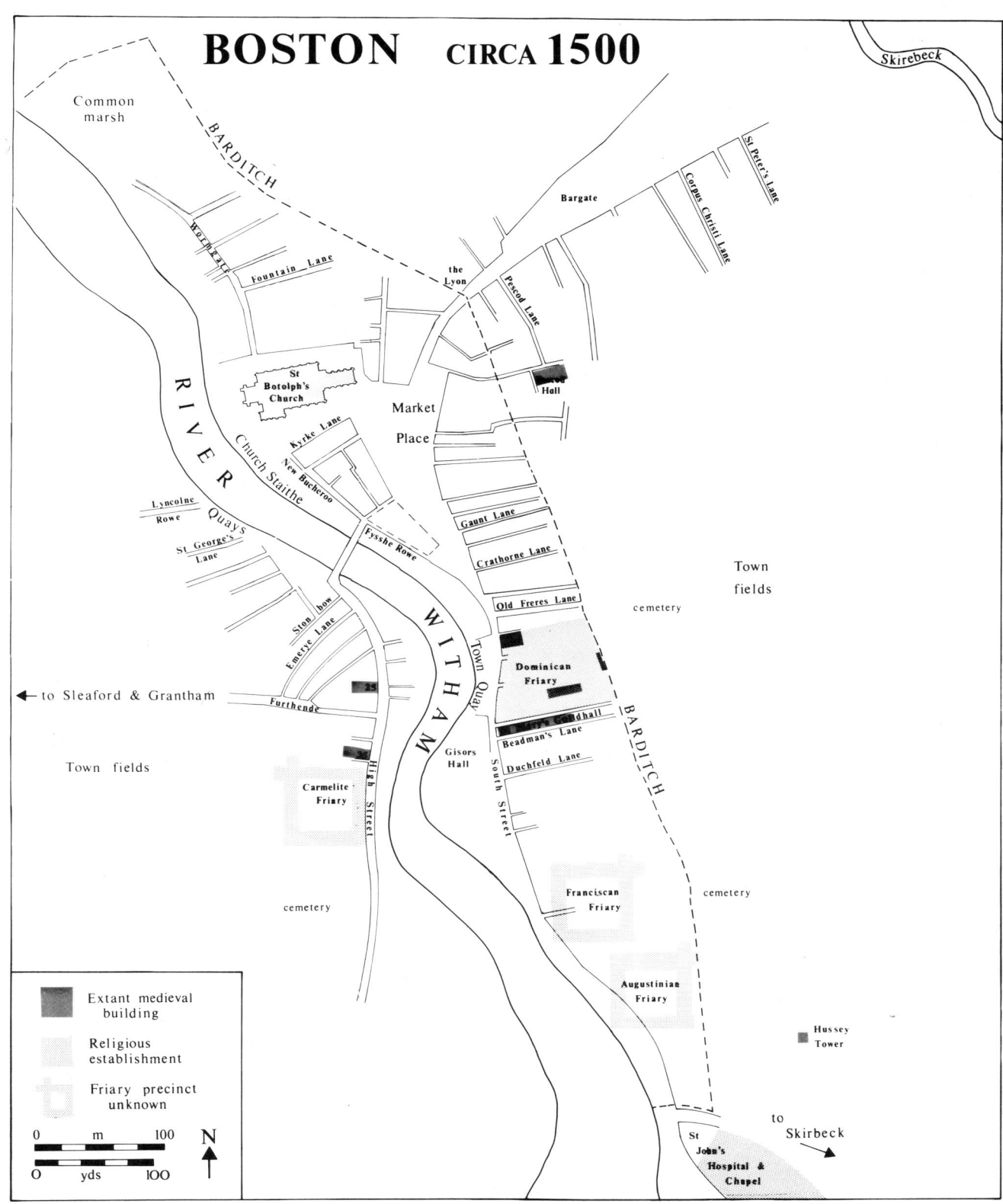

Fig. 9 *A plan of Boston circa A.D. 1500*

403-417), in the medieval and post-medieval periods. To keep the ditch comparatively clean in the sixteenth century it was made to ebb and flood with the tide (*Boston Corp. Mins.* 1561) and each frontage onto the Barditch had to scour it and carry away the filth (*Boston Corp. Mins.* 1567; 1569). Similar provisions may have been made in the medieval period but no record survives.

Wormgate

North of the Church and the churchyard, Wormgate followed the meandering course of the Witham. Various religious houses held property in the street, but the significance and extent of this concentration of religious lands is not fully understood. Those which held property included Fountains Abbey, having *le Poll* with two mills upon it (*Charter Rolls* 1226-1257 336), Malton Priory (BM Cotton Claudius D XI), Barlings Abbey (*Letters and Papers* 1545 no. 846, 87) and Kyme Priory (*Boston Corp. Mins.* 1602). Bridlington, Whitby and Stainfield may also have had properties in Wormgate (BM Add MS 40008; Thompson 1856 212). Fountain Lane on the east side of Wormgate is named after Fountains Abbey, but the origin of the name Wormgate itself is not known.

By the sixteenth century the name *le Poll* had been transferred to the northern gowt of the Barditch, *Dipple Goate* (LAO Misc Don 169). Various tenements in Wormgate are named in the documents of this century, including *Wayne House,* the *Hanging Sword,* the *Old Scole House* and Trinity Hall (*Boston Corp. Mins.* 1571; 1577; 1570; Boston Mun. Bdgs. 4A/1/3).

Bargate

To the north-east of the Market Place, the main street passed over the Barditch into the area where the horse market was held (LRS 46 27) and where urban expansion had begun. The horse mart continued to be held in Bargate in the post-medieval period (*Boston Corp. Mins.* 1573) as well as the beast and sheep marts, whilst merchandise and fish were sold in the Market Place. This division may have been the continuation of medieval practices, but there is at present no known record of what was sold where in the middle ages in Boston.

Lanes leading from Bargate to the south included St. Peter's Lane (Boston. Mun Bdgs. 4B/4/4) with beadsmen's houses and gardens, Corpus Christi Lane and Pescod Lane (*Boston Corp. Mins.* 1581). The situation of the former two lanes, named after two of the gilds established in Boston in the second half of the fourteenth century (*Patent Rolls* 1396-1399 19; BM Harl. MS 4795; *Patent Rolls* 1348-1350 364) is probably a reflection of the extent to which urban expansion of

20

the thirteenth century had reached. Properties in Bargate in the sixteenth century included a smithy and brewhouse (LRS 24 210), *Cleyley House,* and an inn called the *Lyon* held by St. Mary's gild (LAO Misc. Don. 169).

The Bridge and the Market Place

The centre of the settlement of Boston was around the bridge across the Witham, possibly built in 1142 when the sluice was constructed (LAO Monson 7/27). The earliest indication that a bridge existed, however, is not until about 1220, when a shop in *Briggestrathe* is mentioned (LAO MCD 234). In 1316, the *Close Rolls* (1313-1318 369) record that the bailiffs of Boston had illegally placed a drawbridge and barriers at the centre of the bridge and that they were to be removed. During this century the bridge appears to have been in bad repair, for there were several *pontage* and *pavage* grants (*Patent Rolls* 1300-1350). In certain instances these were abused for personal gain, for de Ros had his patent rescinded in 1318 as the bridge was not in disrepair. Two centuries later, after the building of a sluice in the Witham at Boston, by Mayhake of Flanders (LAO Monson 7/27), the bridge itself fell down and had to be totally rebuilt (*Boston Corp. Mins.* 1556).

Briggestrathe led into the Market Place, to which the earliest known reference occurs in the early thirteenth century (LAO MCD 234). Small lanes left the main street to the east and west, but the names of these alleyways, apart from *Monkslane,* are not recorded until the later medieval period (LAO 3 Anc 2/1).

East of the Market Place

In the fifteenth century the lanes which led from the Market Place to the ends of the messuage plots and the Barditch were: *Old Freres Lane,* (Shodfriars Lane), and *Crathorne Lane,* and probably *le Chekker, Chamber Lane, Gascoyne Lane, Tilney Lane* and *Herwood Lane. Chapman Lane, Belton Lane, Bell Lane, Gaunt Lane* and *Tumby Place* may also have been situated off the Market Place, (Boston Mun. Bdgs. Corpus Christi Rental; PRO DL 29 and SC 6; *Close Rolls* 1450-1460 248-9) but these names have not continued in use and their true location cannot, therefore, be identified.

St. Botolph's Church

The earliest reference to St. Botolph's Church has been discussed on page 8, but few details concerning the actual fabric of the early church have been discovered, apart from the fact that Boston parishioners had to fence their churchyard in 1298 (LRS 64 113). The new parish church was built during the fourteenth and early

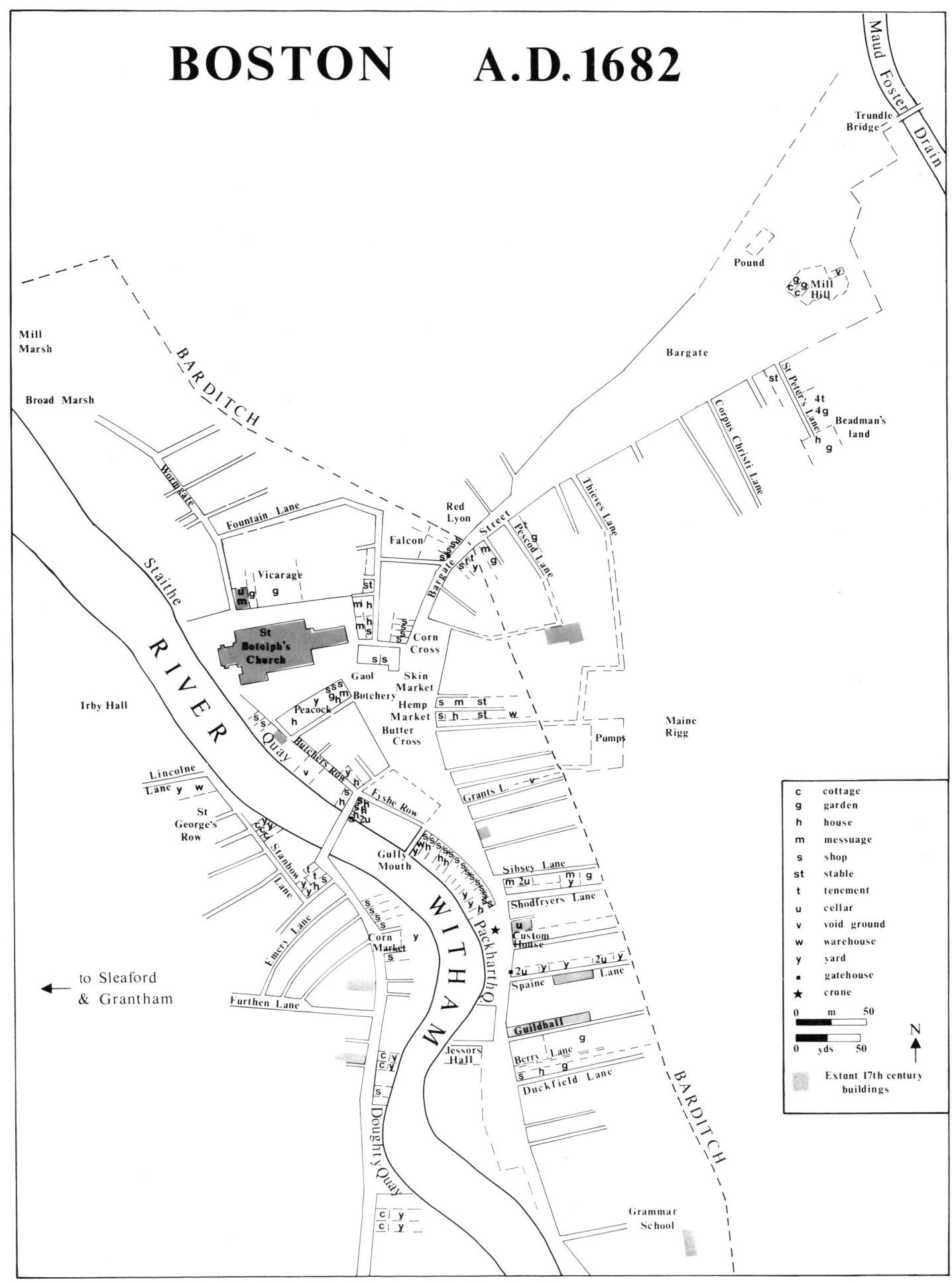

BOSTON A.D. 1682

Maud Foster Drain

Trundle Bridge

Pound

Mill Marsh

Broad Marsh

BARDITCH

Bargate

Mill Hill

Corpus Christi Lane

St Peter's Lane

Beadman's land

Staithe

Wormgate

Fountain Lane

Vicarage

Red Lyon

Falcon

Bargate Street

Pescod Lane

Thieves Lane

RIVER

Irby Hall

St Botolph's Church

Corn Cross

Skin Market

Gaol

Butchery

Hemp Market

Butter Cross

Maine Rigg

Pumps

Quay

Peacock

Butchers Row

Lincolne Lane

Fyshe Row

Grants L.

St George's Row

Stanbow Lane

Gully Mouth

Sibsey Lane

Shodfryers Lane

Custom House

Emery Lane

Corn Market

WITHAM

Spaine Lane

Packhart Qu.

Crane

Guildhall

Furthen Lane

to Sleaford & Grantham

Jessors Hall

Berry Lane

Duckfield Lane

BARDITCH

Doughty Quay

Grammar School

c	cottage
g	garden
h	house
m	messuage
s	shop
st	stable
t	tenement
u	cellar
v	void ground
w	warehouse
y	yard
▪	gatehouse
★	crane

0 m 50

0 yds 50

N

Extant 17th century buildings

Fig. 10 *A plan of Boston A.D. 1681*

21

fifteenth centuries, apparently enclosing the original church. During restoration work in the 1850's, foundations of a small stone church were discovered about 1.25m below the present floor (Jebb 1903 35). Several extensions to the churchyard between 1320 and 1350 allowed for the construction of the very large nave and aisles of the present St. Botolph's (*Patent Rolls* 1317-1321 561; *Ibid* 1340-1343 481; *Ibid* 1345-1348 74).

West of the Market Place

As yet, little is known about the layout of the lanes in the medieval period west of the Market Place. The maps of Boston of the eighteenth and nineteenth centuries indicate that there was considerable rebuilding and clearance in the area between 1741 and 1887. This redevelopment had probably begun before Hall's map of Boston was drawn, for records indicate that there were once several lanes south-east of the town bridge. In the fifteenth century north of the bridge were the *New Bucheroo, Flesheware Rowe, les Barber Rowe* and *Kyrke Lane*. To the south of the bridge were *Fysshe Rowe, Bocher Rowe* and *Conysgate*.

South of the Market Place

The main street south of the Market Place lay parallel to the river as far as St. John's Hospital, outside the Barditch, where the road turned south-east to Skirbeck. Within the Barditch, land does not appear to have been built upon until it was granted to the Dominican and Franciscan Friars, as discussed on page 18.

Dominican Friary

The Dominican Friary was originally built some time during the second half of the thirteenth century, but it had to be rebuilt between 1288 and 1309 after a fire had destroyed much of it (Dugdale 1817 vi 1486). Housing twenty-nine friars in 1300 (Knowles 1971 215), the precinct buildings covered quite a large area between Shodfriars Lane and the surviving Guildhall, the main street and the Barditch.

Part of a large stone building with a series of pointed arches still stands at the northern edge of the precinct near Shodfriars Lane (Fig. 11). It is assumed that this building formed part of the friary, but nothing is known of its function (Plate I). The friary church was probably to the south of this building, possibly extending eastwards as far as the Barditch, for, when the Barditch was repiped in 1976, a masonry wall with a series of buttresses was found to be reinforcing the side of the ditch in this area. The church itself had a nave and choir divided by an entrance to the cloister and another to the street. Above these doorways and the passage between them were the tower and belfry, from which

Plate I *Stone arch within 10 South Street; fourteenth century?*

the friars protected their church and rights of burial against the Bishop of Lincoln in 1376 (Hinnebusch 1951 141). Part of the friary still remains in Spain Lane: the upper storey provided private chambers for certain friars (Plate II). The cloister was in the area to the north of this building, indicating that Spain Lane, which now runs directly in front of Blackfriars, was not in this position in the medieval period. If a lane had existed in the vicinity it would have either been to the south, between the precinct wall and the later Guildhall, or to the north, giving a central entrance to the friary. The cemetery of the Dominican friars was to the east of the precinct on the opposite side of the Barditch, (skeletons were uncovered in Shodfriars Lane in 1964 and 1976).

As well as providing for the religious needs of some of the inhabitants of Boston, the Dominican friars also built a water conduit from Bolingbroke, 35 km away, to the town for their own and the public's use. (*Patent Rolls* 1327-1330 182). This throws some light on one of the sources of fresh water for Boston, for it may have been difficult to obtain unpolluted water in the town, situated as it was on a tidal river close to the sea.

Unlike the other friaries in Boston, the Dominican friary was not granted to the burgesses when the town was given its charter in 1545 (*Letters and Papers* 1545

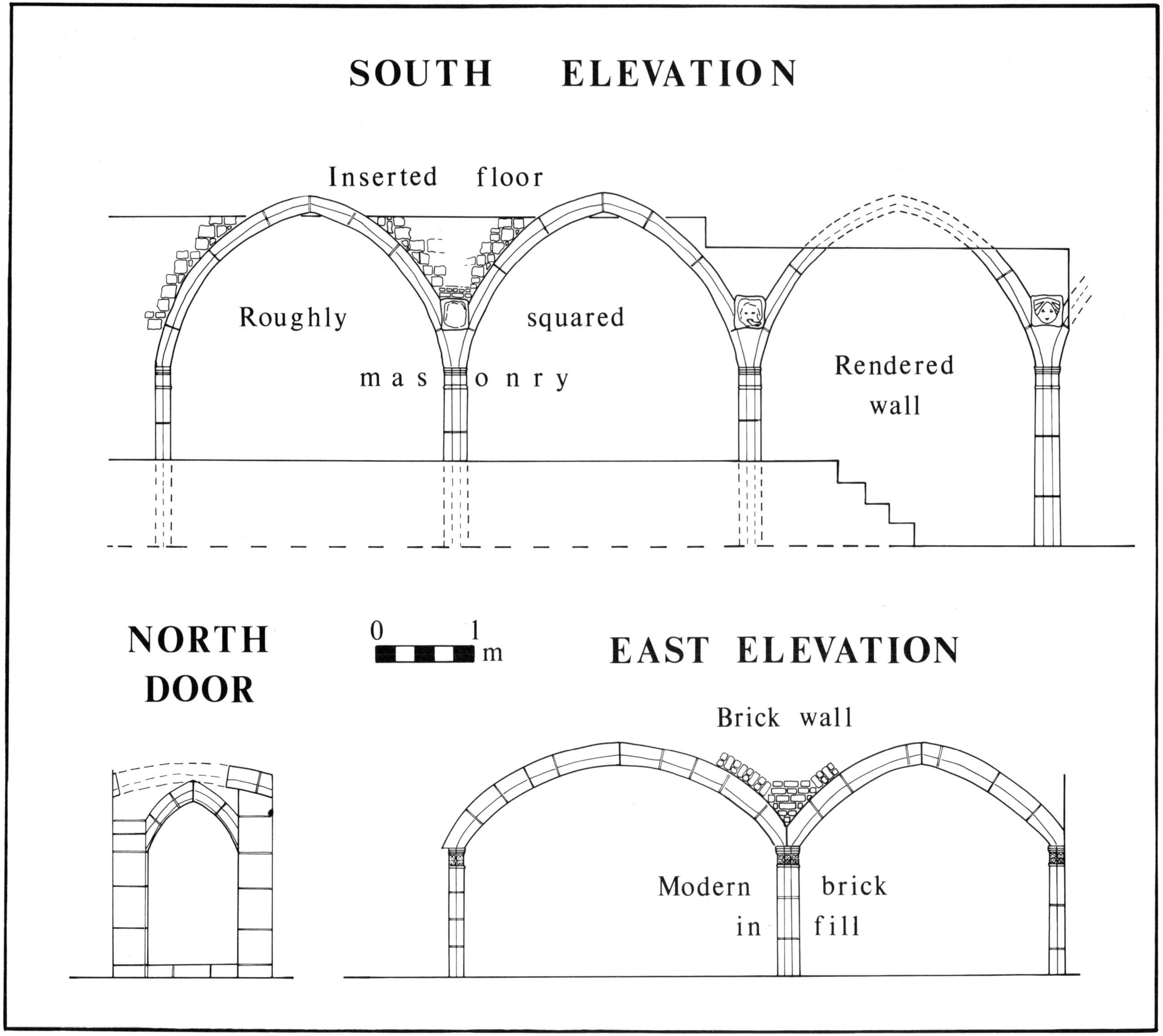

SOUTH ELEVATION

Inserted floor

Roughly

s q u a r e d   m a s o n r y

Rendered
wall

NORTH
DOOR

0 ▮▮▮▮ 1
m

EAST ELEVATION

Brick wall

Modern

brick

in

fill

Fig. 11. Medieval masonry within 10 South Street

no. 846, 87). Most of the precinct buildings apparently survived until the nineteenth century when the front of one of the buildings was demolished, (in 1820) and a fire destroyed other structures, (Thompson 1856 231-232).

Plate II   *Blackfriars, part of the Dominican Friary; built about A.D. 1300.*

St. Mary's Guildhall

In the fifteenth century beside the river, opposite the Dominican Friary, there were staithes, including one against the mansion of the gilds called *Goldenhows.* This reference to St. Mary's Guildhall (Plate III) occurs in the Corpus Christi gild rental. The two gilds may have combined funds to build a hall in the middle of the fifteenth century, but the *compotus* of St. Mary's gild specifically lists all the goods within the hall as being its own property (Boston Mun. Bdgs. 4.A/2.1). The association between these gilds is, therefore, not fully understood. Corpus Christi gild and St. Mary's gild were the most important gilds in the town, owning property in Boston and in nearby villages. The latter gild owned property in *Flesherowe*, Wormgate, *Raton Rowe*, Bargate and *Forthende*, as well as Beadman's Lane south of the Guildhall, (LAO Misc. Don. 169).

South End

There appear to be no documentary references to this area of Boston until the second half of the fifteenth and sixteenth centuries when, to the south of St. Mary's

Guildhall, there was *Duchfeld Lane* and various tenements including *le Christophre, Redman's Place* and *Cornerplace,* the latter being situated in *Quykerrellane* or *Garnounlane* (*Close Rolls* 1437-1439 339). *Gisors Hall,* the weigh-house of Boston, stood south-west of the Guildhall, beside the Witham (Thompson 1856 236). Some of the masonry from this building has been re-used in the ground floor of Hurst's in South Square (Plate IV).

Plate III   *St Mary's Guildhall; circa A.D. 1450.*

24

Franciscan Friary

Although its exact location is not known, the Franciscan Friary stood close to where the present Grammar School is now located. Parts of a large cemetery of the Grey Friars were discovered when the school was extended and playing fields were laid out, and during commercial excavations in Rowley Road (skeletons were discovered in 1959, 1967 and 1975). The gravestone of Wisselus de Smalenburg had already been removed from the site to the parish church where it can still be seen. The friars owned six acres of pasture east of the Barditch in this vicinity, west of the Maud Foster Drain and north of Hussey Tower (Boston Mun. Bdgs. 4.A.1/37), but the nature of the precinct buildings on the west side of the Barditch are not mentioned in the relevant documents. The earliest reference to the Franciscan friary occurs in 1268, when wine and goods left in their church were stolen (VCH 1906 215).

Augustinian Friary

The site of this friary is not known, except that it was in the south of the town to the east of the Witham. The area that is indicated as the site of the Augustinian Friary on the 2½″ O.S. map of the vicinity is south-east of the Barditch, in what was then Skirbeck. Doubts as to the validity of this theory can be expressed by the following consideration. St. John's Hospital, which was sited south-east of the Barditch, was consistently described as being in *Skirbeck by Boston*, whereas the Augustinian Friary was the Austin Friary *of Boston*. This suggests that the site was not outside the Barditch, but was within it, possibly adjacent to the Franciscan Friary.

The friary was established during the second decade of the fourteenth century, and there are several references in the *Patent Rolls* to grants of land being made to the Augustinians, for the erection of a dwelling house, at this time. However, there are indications that the mendicants were having difficulties in maintaining their prosperity, for in 1456 the Tilney family of Boston were granted a pasture in the Friars Austin in Boston (*Close Rolls* 1447-1456 248). As with the Franciscan and Carmelite friaries, the Augustinian friary was granted to the borough of Boston in 1545 (*Letters and Papers* 1545 no. 846, 87), and was subsequently rented out as pasture, (*Boston Corp. Mins.* 1559; 1564).

South of the Barditch

Hussey Tower, part of the living quarters of a late fifteenth century manor house, is situated outside the Barditch and south of the Franciscan Friary cemetery (Plate V). South-east of the Barditch was the Hospital of St. John of Jerusalem, with its church, which was established by 1220 (LRS 3 115). The chuchyard is still visible beside the road to Skirbeck, but the church fell into disrepair in the 1500's and was pulled down in 1583 (*Boston Corp. Mins.* 1583). Tradition says that the *Hansa stilyard* was also in this part of Skirbeck (Dover 1970 20). There is no evidence to support the theory, except that by the 1300's there would have been little land available beside the Witham, other than in this vicinity, on which the *Hansa* could build its house, warehouse and quay.

Plate V   *Hussey Tower; circa A.D. 1450.* (*C. R. Theobald*)

West of the Witham

For the west side of the river there are very few documentary references until the late medieval period. Settlement was probably near the bridge, extending approximately 100m north and south of it, but little is known of the layout of the lanes in the area. Hall's map of 1741 shows some property boundaries and lanes that have medieval characteristics; they are long and narrow, lying east-west to the main street. The only lane that can be positively identified as having been in existence in the thirteenth century, however, is *Stonbow*, where Crowland Abbey held land (LAO FLMSS 7). Lincoln Lane may be named after the Lincoln merchants who apparently built properties of stone in the vicinity in the late 1200's, (Thompson 1856 41).

This part of Boston, on the west side of the river, was apparently not within the Richmond fee. The families of de Croun and de Tatteshall held fees in this area in the medieval period (*Hundred Rolls* i. 348-350) but topographical details of the differences, if any, resulting from having two major landholders are yet to be discovered.

North-west of the Bridge

In the late fifteenth century, opposite the church, were *Stonbow* or Stanbow Lane and *Lyncolne Row* in which *Newlands Place* stood (Boston Mun. Bdg. Corpus Christi rental). St. Mary's gild appears to have owned a series of properties in the area, for twelve cottages were built for the gild in the row in the late 1400's (LAO Misc. Don 169). Staithes lined the Witham at the end of Lincoln Row opposite the *Church Staithe* on the east bank (*Boston Corp. Mins.* 1582).

South-west of the Bridge

South of the bridge, leading to the west were *Emerye Lane* and *Furthende*, the latter finally becoming West Street in the early nineteenth century. There are two medieval timber-framed halls still standing at 25 and 35 High Street, dating from the fifteenth century (Plates VI, VII and VIII and Fig. 12).

Carmelite Friary

South of these extant medieval buildings was the Carmelite Friary. The church and house were built of brick, tile and stone, (*Boston Corp. Mins.* 1560), sometime after 1293 (*Patent Rolls* 1307--1313 17; Knowles 1971 234), but the extent of the friary precinct is not known.

Plate VI   35 *High Street; a nineteenth century facade.*

Plate VII   35 *High Street, the north wall; probably fifteenth century.*

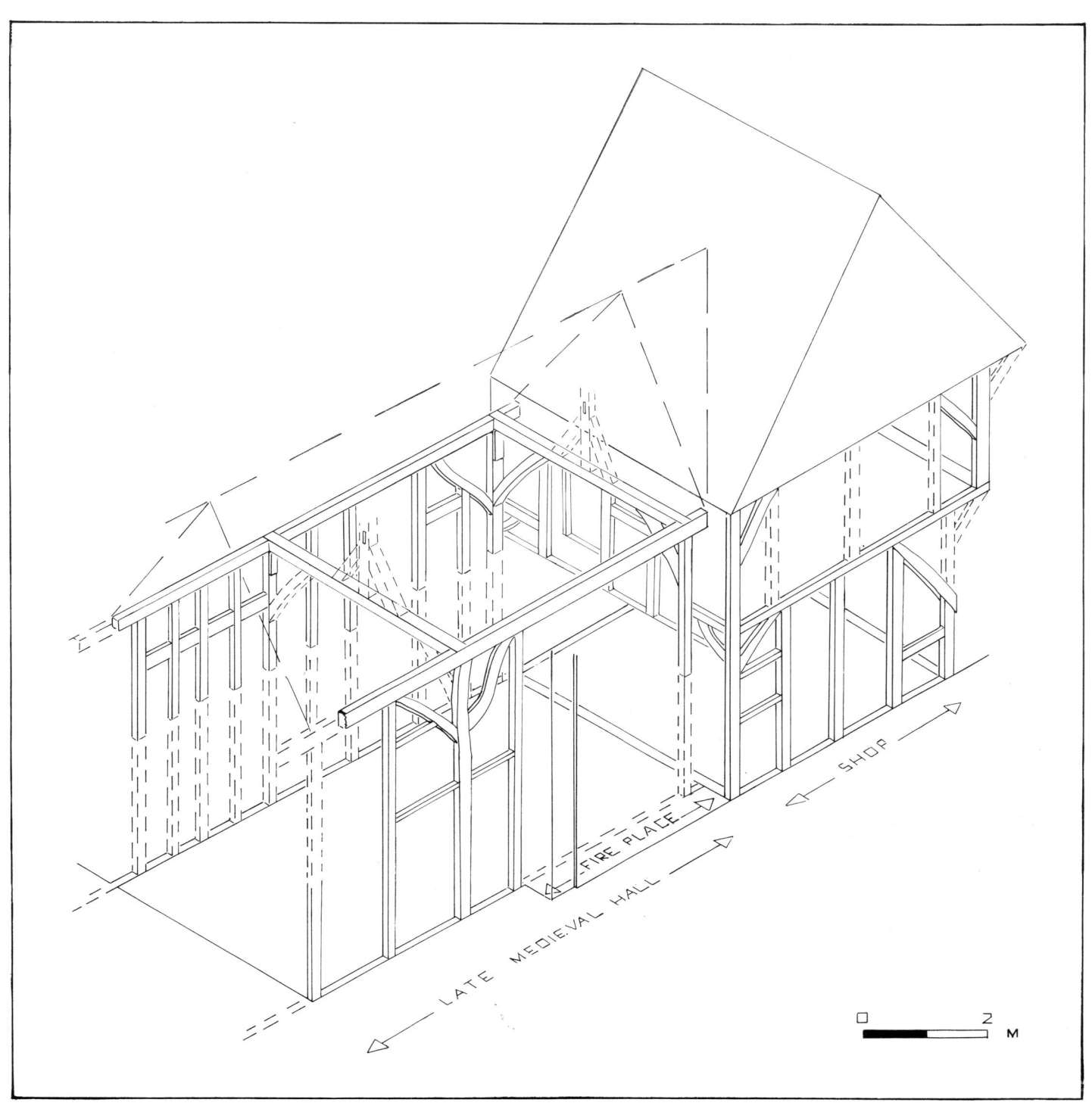

Fig. 12 *A reconstruction of the medieval timber framed building at 25 High Street*

Town fields and reclamation

At present very little is known about the town fields of Boston, except for certain names recorded in the sixteenth century — *Broadfield* and *Butgate* (*Boston Corp. Mins.* 1563; 1601) *Westnam Thynge* and *Grenedyke* (*Letters and Papers* 1545 no. 846, 87). There is also comparatively little known of land reclamation from the sea and the fens around Boston until the post-medieval period. Commissions of banking and dyking were established in the fourteenth century (*Patent Rolls*) but details of their work are not recorded until the sixteenth century (LRS 54; 63; Hallam 1965).

Plate VIII   25 *High Street; late fifteenth century upper floor.*

Conclusion

This survey of the topography of Boston in the medieval period is obviously incomplete. There are areas of the town which are inadequately recorded and many references which cannot be located on a plan of the town. The latter include *Barkerhowses* and *Strawstonhows* on the west side of the Witham (Boston Mun. Bdg. Corpus Christi rental), *Coypitte* east of the Barditch (*Close Rolls* 1460-1465 152), the *Greneyard* (*Inq. Post Mort* 1317 48), *Leydenhalle* (*Close Rolls* 1385-1389 566), *le Mothalle* and *le Northhalle* (*Inq Post Mort* 1306 391). It is also evident that many of the lanes cannot be accurately planned, as shown by the long list of lanes possibly situated on the east side of the Market Place, (page 20).

It is not known what was built on plots of land in medieval Boston, except from isolated documentary sources and the few extant buildings of the period. A plot of land with a bakehouse is noted, and land with buildings and a staithe which had to be maintained (LAO 3 Anc 2/1). Apart from these references there is no information as yet for Boston itself. Useful parallels can, however, be drawn from extant buildings in King's Lynn (Parker 1971) and from archaeological excavations in Southampton (Platt 1975) and elsewhere. These plots of land are described as *messuagium*, *tenementum* and *curia*, the meanings of which cannot be easily elucidated by a Latin-English translation, although they occur frequently in documents relating to property in the medieval and post-medieval periods. *Messuagium* and *tenementum* were used when referring to properties or plots of land, but whether the terms were used to describe two different types of property or the mode of tenure of that land is not yet known. Further research is required before the question — what was a *messuagium*? can be answered.

Some details of the size of properties held in the middle ages are given in certain documents, particularly the Huntingfield cartulary (LAO 3Anc 2/1), and a general concept of their shape can be gained from the extant examples of boundaries in the town. Plots of land that are mentioned include one 100 ft. by 24 ft., another 180 ft. by 24 ft. and others 50 ft. and 57 ft. in length. There is also reference to a lane 7 ft. wide, but it is not named. Other properties are described elsewhere; Barlings Abbey held land 89 ft. long by 30 ft. wide (LAO MF 101), extending to the *Bardyke*, and Alvingham Priory held property 24 ft. wide by 31 ft. long (LAO MF 100).

It is evident that the division of plots of land had begun by the late twelfth and early thirteenth centuries. Areas of land were apparently being granted to various people from a larger unit, the *curia,* or courtyard, (LAO 3 Anc 2/1). This is presumably indicative of population pressure on the available land, but the usage of the term is not fully understood. In the fourteenth century there are certain references to the leasing of void land in the town, presumably indicative of a decrease in population and, probably, trade. These occur in 1335, when void plots which were held by the Richmond fee for the erection of stalls at fair time are mentioned (*Inq Post Mort* 426) and in 1364 when the Earl of Richmond leased void land in the south end of Boston (*Patent Rolls* 1361-1364 517). These appear to be in contrast to the early thirteenth century records, mentioned above.

Later topographical references also seem to indicate that there may have been a decline in the prosperity of the town, although they may be biased accounts to relieve Boston of certain taxes due. Various comments were made on the decay and dangers of the river Witham (*Letters and Papers* 1537 no. 77) and a survey of the repairs needed to be made to the King's tenements and staithes was made in 1539 (*Ibid* 1539 no. 342).

Many other features of Boston's topography are not apparent from extant remains or documentary sources. Archaeological excavation and further research may throw some light on the following topographical problems:— Did Boston develop naturally as a market town and port or was it planned as such by one of the major landholders in the vicinity, such as the Earl of Richmond? What effects did three major landholders in Boston have on the topography of the town? What were the different modes of tenure in Boston?

Historic Buildings in Boston

Buildings and Planning

Most of the centre of Boston now forms part of a Conservation Area (Fig. 2) under which all buildings are treated as Listed if an application is made to demolish them. Approval of the Planning Department has to be sought and the matter has to be advertised to the public. If approval is given, the owner is obliged by law to notify the Royal Commission on Historical Monuments. Unless the building is of outstanding importance, the work load of the Commission is such that only a photographic record is made. These are kept in the National Monuments Record at the Department of the Environment, Fortress House, 23 Savile Row, London W1X 1AB.

Plate IX   82 *High Street; a seventeenth century timber framed house.*

It is imperative that an expert is available to examine all buildings to be demolished, whether they are Listed or not. The Department of the Environment's List of Buildings of Special Architectural or Historic Interest for Boston was revised in 1975. This lists over 300 buildings, the majority being Grade II, although there are some Grade II* and Grade I. Unfortunately, the survey was largely done by looking at the exterior of the buildings in the town, rather than a detailed interior examination. This has resulted in the Listing of the facade rather than the actual construction.

Plate X   127 *High Street; a seventeenth century timber framed building.*

Thus a fifteenth century timber framed hall and the later shop at the front at 35 High Street has not been included on the List, (Plate VII). The timber framed seventeenth century building at 82 High Street also fails to appear on the List, (Plate IX). Others have been incorrectly identified. The late eighteenth century house with a nineteenth century bay window at 127 High Street turned out to be a timber framed building of the

Plate XI   127 *High Street, in process of demolition; one of the main vertical timbers is visible on the left of the photograph.*

mid 1600's when it was demolished (Plate X). In the Market Place, numbers 27 and 28 are timber framed of the seventeenth century rather than of the 1700's (Plate XII). Further examples of the inaccuracies of the List could be given, but these serve as indications that a detailed examination of all buildings should be made.

There are few buildings of the medieval period surviving in Boston, so that every effort should be made to preserve those that do remain. Those known to have been built before A.D. 1500 are as follows:—
35 High Street; 25 High Street; St. Botolph's Church; Pescod Hall; the masonry contained within 10 South Street; part of the Dominican Friary in Spain Lane; the Guildhall in South Street; Hussey Tower, north of Skirbeck Road.

Plate XII   27 *and* 28 *Market Place; timber framed of the seventeenth century, or possibly earlier.*

This group of known medieval buildings might be extended if a detailed survey of houses in the centre of Boston was made. Associated with such a project could be the recording of the types of materials used in construction in different periods and the varied size and number of rooms of a building, as in the survey of historic buildings of Bedfordshire (1975), compiled by the County's Planning Department.

Other features of the medieval period should also be preserved, but there is no policy to do so, nor are there any legal provisions for their protection. These are the street pattern, lanes and property boundaries of medieval Boston. They are visible features of the past that are all too often forgotten when planning applications are considered, particularly that of the property boundary.

Building materials

Indications of the materials used in building are widespread for the post-medieval period. Well over ninety per cent of the buildings in the centre of Boston date from the eighteenth century to the present day. The most common building material was, and still is, brick, mainly locally produced until fairly recently. Most of the old brick pits have now been filled in, but they existed to the north of the present station yard, between George Street and High Street, between Sleaford Road and the South Forty Foot Drain, and to the east of Brothertoft Lane. The bricks were used in the construction of buildings such as Fydell House (Plate XIII), the Custom House (Plate XIV), and Old Church House (Plate XV).

Plate XIII   *Fydell House, South Street; completed A.D. 1724.*

Plate XIV   *Custom House, South Street; circa A.D. 1720.*

able distance from Boston of the limestone quarries at Ancaster and in the Stamford region. Similar problems of supply were encountered with the demand for timbers and thus other sources of material were tapped that could be locally produced. Stone was used, however, for decorative architraves and wall angles, and reused from medieval buildings in 10 South Street (Plate XVII) and Hurst's warehouse, South Square (Plate IV).

Roofing materials of the sixteenth century to the present day consisted of clay tiles, either pantiles or plain tiles, and slates. The burgesses of the borough refused to allow thatch to be used after the sixteenth century because of the fire risk (*Boston Corp Mins.* 1606).

By the seventeenth century the use of timbers as major structural supports was on the decline and where they were used they were generally of poor quality, reused medieval timbers, or less substantial deal beams rather than oak. There are several examples of timber framed buildings of the seventeenth century, including Key Studio (Plate XVI) and 27-28 Market Place (Plate XII), with an infilling of brick between the frame. There is no evidence at present in Boston that mud and stud was used during this period as an infill and cover to the frame.

Stone was not used for construction purposes in Boston in the post-medieval period until the Assembly Rooms and the major banks' premises were built in the nine-teenth century. This was probably due to the consider-

Plate XV   *Old Church House, Wormgate; seventeenth century*

Plate XVI   *Key Studio, Church Lane; seventeenth century.*

Little is known of the building materials used in the medieval period in Boston and nothing at all is known of housing in the eleventh and twelfth centuries. Timber framed buildings were being built in the fourteenth century, with oak supplied from Sherwood Forest (*Close Rolls* 1288-1296 102) and Hastings (*Patent Rolls* 1385-1389 306) in certain instances. Other sources of supply are not known.

Stone was used for more substantial buildings, such as St. Botolph's Church and the Dominican Friary which are extant, and the Lincoln merchants' houses on the west side of the river, (Thompson 1856 41). However, there must have been problems with supply, (as in the post-medieval period) making the use of stone very expensive.

Bricks were being made in Boston as early as the late thirteenth century, for they form the kiln for the firing of clay roof tiles (Mayes 1965), but it is not known to what extent they were produced for house building at this time. They were being made on a larger scale by the 1430's in Boston, for Tattershall Castle (LRS 55 60) was supplied with bricks from the town.

Other building materials can only be conjectured until archaeological excavation reveals remains of medieval buildings. Turves, thatch, reeds and mud and stud may all have been used with wood for constructing homes, but there is no known documentary source or existing building in Boston recording their use. It is also not known in what proportions the three major materials, timber, stone and brick, were used and whether or not their use was restricted to the properties of certain ranks of society. Archaeological excavation could help to answer these problems.

Plate XVII   10 *South Street; a nineteenth century facade with reused masonry for ornamentation.*

Medieval Buildings in Boston

The form of building of the middle ages in Boston is not known, except for Pescod Hall (Plate XVIII) and two much altered examples of late medieval box timber framed constructions at 25 and 35 High Street (Plates VI, VII and VIII). These latter two buildings are set with the longest side of the hall at right angles to the street front (Fig. 12). They consist of a hall, which is open to the roof and a front shop, with a chamber above and an attic in the roof. Access to these upper storeys was probably by a ladder from the hall. The timber framed shop at 25 High Street may be of a more recent date than the hall behind, for the two parts of the building do not marry together. There is evidence to suggest that the shop facade was jettied at two levels, a characteristic also indicating a late, rather than early fifteenth century building. The hall was later divided into two storeys by inserting a floor. Subsequent alterations in the eighteenth and nineteenth centuries have removed the hall roof altogether in 25 High Street and inserted a third storey to the shop front at 35 High Street.

Little light can be shed on the general standard of these buildings, the class of person who lived in them, or how many people dwelled in the house at one time. One can gain some impression of the dwellings that existed in Boston in the medieval period by comparison with the other Fenland towns which have more survivals and have had excavations, such as King's Lynn (Parker 1971), or by research into documentary sources for the sixteenth century. There are few documentary references to buildings, but post-medieval probate inventories are useful, listing the contents of each room at the death of the owner. There are many of these available for inhabitants of Boston. The details of their homes vary from those living in a house consisting of a hall and kitchen, to those with a hall, parlour, kitchen, chamber, shop and workshop or warehouse. John, tiler of Boston in the 1540's, had property in the hall, great chamber, kitchen, chamber over the parlour of the north part of the hall, the parlour under the same, the chamber on the buttery and the buttery. (LAO INV 13/21). Ultimately, however, it is the archaeologist who can discover most about the medieval buildings of Boston by excavation.

Plate XVIII   *Pescod Hall, Mitre Lane; circa A.D. 1450, restored.*

Archaeology in Boston

Archaeological Deposits

The continuous settlement of Boston from at least the twelfth century over a small area has resulted in the accumulation of archaeological deposits, as houses and lanes have been renewed. The ground level has, therefore, risen since the medieval period. As very few excavations have been carried out in Boston it is not certain to what depth these layers reach, but medieval pottery has been discovered in several instances at least 2m below the present surface to the south of the Market Place. This is not to say that features of the middle ages do not also occur at depths of 1m or less in other parts of the medieval town.

Thus, any redevelopment in the centre of Boston that has foundations of 1m or more depth will probably destroy archaeological material. Much of the destruction of archaeological deposits in Boston occurred in the eighteenth and nineteenth centuries, with the construction of cellars. Only the very deepest levels will have survived and, therefore, such sites may not warrant intensive archaeological work. As a preliminary to archaeological rescue excavations a survey of the buildings with cellars has been compiled. This has been deposited with the South Lincolnshire Archaeological Unit as an aid towards assessing the archaeological potential of a site. Such a survey has its drawbacks, however, for many cellars have since been filled in, often leaving little trace in the present building.

Twentieth century redevelopment has tended to be on an even larger scale than during the eighteenth and nineteenth centuries. For this reason archaeological information should be recovered before further areas of the medieval town are damaged or destroyed by constructions such as the Classic Cinema, South Square; Marks and Spencers, Market Place; Woolworths, Strait Bargate; the Police Station, Lincoln Lane; and new road schemes.

Archaeology and Redevelopment

Redevelopment in Boston will, presumably, continue at a similar rate as in the recent past. This has included two major areas of construction and various small developments, none of which have been adequately recorded by archaeologists. The redevelopment around Lincoln Lane was not observed by archaeologists and opportunities were lost to investigate the medieval merchants' houses and quays along 200m of the adjoining river bank. The Inner Relief Road has cut through the supposed site of the Franciscan Friary, and the medieval town boundary, the Barditch. The

access to this new road has destroyed archaeological deposits at the back of the properties lying between the Market Place and the Barditch without sufficient detailed recording of the levels removed.

Developments in the future include the construction of further buildings around Lincoln Lane and the dual carriageway at the south end of High Street. Small rebuilding programmes include the enlargement of Boots across the Barditch between Grants Lane and Craythorne Lane, and the building of a club in Cornhill Lane. These will begin within the next six months, and there will probably be similar planning applications in the coming years. It is hoped that this survey will go some way towards the provision of information for the archaeologist, so that opportunities for archaeological research and rescue excavations will not be missed in the future, as they have been in the past, in Boston.

Archaeology and the Developer

Time is an important factor when dealing with a site that is to be redeveloped. As yet there are no provisions in law to allow sufficient time for an excavation to take place between the demolition of a building and the redevelopment of a site, unless it is scheduled. It is important that archaeological factors are taken into account in the early stages of any planning application, so that no delay is caused to the contractor.

It is, therefore, necessary that all those concerned with redevelopment are aware of the destruction that occurs to our heritage by the very nature of their work. Cooperation should exist between archaeologists, planners, developers and contractors. Appropriate methods should be employed to record features of historic importance and, in selected instances, conserve them. In many cases archaeological excavation in England has only taken place where there is a considerable threat to the layers that exist. Shallow foundations for a road or building may be judged to be sealing the deposits rather than destroying them. A survey enables priorities for detailed archaeological research and excavation to be determined, so that cost effective projects are undertaken by the archaeologist with the co-operation of the developer. Modern society is progressive and change is part of it, but it is imperative that time is taken to record, for future generations, that which we destroy.

Archaeological Policy

The archaeologists in the area should have the resources to take advantage of these redevelopments. At present the main resource which is not available is finance. Archaeological excavation, a necessary part of research if Boston's past is to be discovered, is expensive. In Boston the cost of an excavation is increased by the necessity of shoring the edges of trenches, the subsoil of the town being particularly unstable. Problems will be encountered with the high water table and the use of pumps will be necessary. One excavation in the town would cost at least £5,000, the cost varying with the size of site, special problems, labour, the need for machinery, the types of finds (whether or not they need conservation) and the time taken to excavate and prepare the report on the work. Although this amount of money may seem an expense that can be ill-afforded in the present economic climate, the gain in our knowledge of Boston's past would far out-weigh the problem of financial outlay. So little is known of the everyday life of the inhabitants of the town in the medieval period, as is evident from the historical survey of Boston attempted in previous pages, that archaeologists could provide useful insights into that life.

An area of archaeological importance with good potential should be chosen for excavation. That is, a site without too much disturbance by later developments and of a large enough size for interpretation to be as accurate as possible, considering the problems that are to be faced.

Sites not suitable for excavation should be observed by an archaeologist during redevelopment and features of interest recorded. Although this provides a far from complete record of the site, it can give valuable information as to the period of occupation of that part of the town. It also provides knowledge of the various subsoils which may be encountered. In Boston this could be particularly useful, as soil types which are uncovered vary greatly, as does the occurrence of water-logging.

Priorities for Archaeological Work in Boston

1. Money should be made available to the Archaeological Unit responsible for this area, so that the following can be attempted.

2. All redevelopments should, ideally, be observed by an archaeologist. Watching briefs should not only include sites within the medieval town, but also in the present borough generally. The medieval tile kiln was found outside the Barditch near the Maud Foster Drain and a quantity of Roman pottery was found when Woad Farm Primary School was built, indicating the variety of archaeological material which may be found on the outskirts of the town.

3. The excavation of a riverside site should be undertaken. The site should be one where reclamation from the river has occurred, preserving the quays which lined the Witham in the medieval period. The associated warehouse or house should be excavated with the quay, giving a fairly comprehensive picture of a unit that was vital to the economy of Boston.

4. A shop and house plot should be excavated in the town centre. This would help to establish a stratigraphy for the town and perhaps reveal the function of the premises and the land behind it, provide an example of the types of houses that were being built in Boston throughout the medieval period and their development, the class of inhabitants and their everyday life.

5. The complete excavation of a cross section of the Barditch should take place, to establish the period of its construction and the form of the inner bank.

6. The excavation of other sites, as they are threatened by redevelopment, should not be ruled out. In particular this should occur when a site could help to establish the origins of Boston.

7. Any excavation which is undertaken should be published. Excavation is of no value unless the results are available to everyone.

Glossary

berewic	detached portion of a manor, part of a larger estate (LRS 19)
bovate	1/8 of a carucate (*Ibid*)
carucate	a measure of land, though probably notional in use, it probably averaged about 160 acres (*Ibid*)
demesne	land over which the lord had direct control or special rights (*Ibid*)
fee	that right which a tenant had in lands, to use them and take the profits from them, whilst rendering knight service to the lord (*Pipe Rolls* 1889)
geld	to be accountable for, or to pay, a tax (*Ibid*)
prises	debts of the king
sokeland	land over which a lord had certain rights, especially justice (LRS 19)
sokeman	a holder of sokeland, in various ways dependent on his lord (*Ibid*)
staithe	landing stage
villein	an unfree tenant of a lord (*Ibid*)
wapentake	a Danish term for a sub-division of a shire

1 sack of wool = 364 lbs

The above are general definitions and do not take into account the historical variations of usage during the middle ages, nor the more recent ideas concerning terminology in the medieval period.

Abbreviations

Boston Corp Mins	Boston Corporation Minutes
Boston Mun Bdgs	Boston Municipal Buildings
B.M.	British Museum
East Mid Geog	East Midland Geographer
E.H.R.	English Historical Review
Ec.H.R.	Economic History Review
Geog J	Geographical Journal
Inq Misc	Calendar of Inquisitions Miscellaneous in the PRO
Inq Post Mort	Calendar of Inquisitions Post Mortem in the PRO
J Arch Assoc	Journal of the Archaeological Association
J Geol Soc	Journal of the Geological Society
LAO	Lincolnshire Archive Office
LAASRP	Lincolnshire Architectural and Archaeological Society's Reports and Papers
LHA	Lincolnshire History and Archaeology
LRS	Lincoln Record Society
Linc Hist	Lincolnshire Historian
Med Arch	Medieval Archaeology
PRO	Public Record Office
Plac Capit West	Placitorum in Domo Capitulari Westmonsteriensi
Rot Parl	Rotuli Parliamentorum
Tax Eccl	Taxatio Ecclesiastica
VCH	Victoria County History

Bibliography

Manuscript sources

Boston Municipal Buildings:

Boston Corporation Minutes A.D. 1545— (transcription in progress, J. F. Bailey M.A.)
Original charters of 1545, 1573, 1604, 1685
Rental of the Corpus Christi gild of Boston 1489

1/B/6	Copy of the charter of Philip and Mary (copies of charters 1/B/1-7)
3/J/1.1	Court Leet Book 1678-1689
3/J/1.2	Court Leet Book 1691
3/J/2.A	Rental of accounts of Boston 1564-1565
3/1/2.B.1	Rents of assize of Boston 1674
3/J/2.B.2	Rents of assize of Boston 1681
3/J/2.B.3	Rents of assize of Boston 1700
4/A/1-42	Property title deeds and securities (mainly 1500-1900)
4/A/2.1	Inventory of goods of St. Mary's gild, Boston 1523
4/C/1.1	Compotus of the bailiff of St. Mary's gild, Boston 1525
4/C/1.2	Compotus of the bailiff of St. Mary's gild, Boston 1538
4/B/4.2	Acre Book 1639-1648
4/B/4.4	Acre Book 1678-1681

Boston Library:

L 352 Wheeler W. H. Pamphlets and papers relating to Boston including an Acre Book of Boston 1661-1662
Collection of maps of Lincolnshire and Boston dating from 1610 to 1888.

Boston Guildhall Museum:

Collection of topographical prints of Boston 1700-1900
Small collection of maps of Lincolnshire and Boston 1650-1840

British Museum:

Add MS 4008 Bridlington Priory cartulary
Add MSS 38816 St. Mary's, York, cartulary
Bibl Harl 4795 Corpus Christi gild register and calendar of Boston
Cotton Claudius D.XI Malton Priory register

Lincolnshire Archive Office:

Collection of property title deeds, securities and documents subsidiary to title. These are catalogued under a great variety of headings but are listed in the Archive's record card system under 'Boston'.

Collection of probate inventories listed by box and number, name and town.

Collection of maps which are catalogued under a variety of headings but are listed in the Archive's record card systems of places and maps under 'Boston'.

Misc Dep 273	Skirbeck Quarter Acre Book 1677
Monson 7/27	The sluice at Boston A.D. 1500
3 Anc 2/1	Huntingfield cartulary
Misc Don 169	Compotus of St. Mary's gild, Boston, A.D. 1515
FL MSS p7	Crowland cartulary transcript
MCD 234	Notes on deeds of St Bartholomew's Hospital relating to Boston
MF 100	Microfilm of Alvingham Priory cartulary
MF 101	Microfilm of Barlings Abbey cartulary
Cragg 4/12A	Corpus Christi gild rental
FL MSS p5	Bardney Abbey cartulary transcript
Monson 7/43	Notes on townships in Lincolnshire by Bishop Sanderson A.D. 1641
MF 82	Wrest Park cartulary microfilm
MF 106	Stixwold Priory cartulary microfilm

Public Record Office:

MPC 54	Ancient map of Holland Fen
MPC 212	Lincolnshire and Nottinghamshire A.D. 1576
MPC 207	Lands north of Boston cA.D. 1640
MPH 313	Lincolnshire A.D. 1801
MPC 141	Lynn and Boston Deeps A.D. 1843

DL 29 and SC 6 Ministers' Accounts:
DL 29 639/10376 1-2 Ed IV Accounts of the manor of Boston
SC 6 909/4 19-20 Ric II; 909/5 18-19 Ed IV; 909/23 31-32 Hen VI; 1116/9 23-24 Ed I; 1118/2 18-21 Ed IV; Hen VII 1771; Hen VIII 1905 Accounts of the manor of Boston

Primary Sources:

Assize Rolls of Lincolnshire 1202-1209 ed D. M. Stenton LRS 22 1926
A Lincolnshire Assize Roll 1298 ed W. S. Thompson LRS 36 1944
Building Accounts of Tattershall Castle 1434-1472 ed W. D. Simpson LRS 55 1960
Calendar of Chancery Warrants preserved in the Public Record Office 1244-1326 London 1927
Calendar of the various Chancery Rolls preserved in the Public Record Office 1277-1326 London 1912
Calendar of Charter Rolls preserved in the Public Record Office 6 vols London 1903-1927
Calendar of Close Rolls preserved in the Public Record Office London 1892- (in progress)
Calendar of Fine Rolls preserved in the Public Record Office London 1911- (in progress)
Calendar of Inquisitions Miscellaneous (Chancery) preserved in the Public Record Office London 1916- (in progress)
Calendar of Inquisitions Post Mortem and other analogous documents preserved in the Public Record Office Henry VII 3 vols London 1898-1955
Calendar of Patent Rolls preserved in the Public Record Office London 1891- (in progress)
Calendarium Genealogicum Hen III and Ed I London 1865
Calendarum Rotulorum Chartarum et Inquisitiones ad quod damnum Record Commissioners London 1803
Calendarum Rotulorum Patentium Record Commissioners London 1802
Close Rolls of the reign of Henry III preserved in the Public Record Office 14 vols London 1902-1938
Curia Regis Rolls A.D. 1196-1237 *preserved in the Public Record Office* 15 vols London 1922-1964
Early Lincoln Wills ed. A. Gibbons Lincoln 1888
Excerpta e Rotulis Finium Record Commissioners London 1835
Feudal Aids A.D. 1284-1431 *preserved in the Public Record Office* 6 vols London 1899-1920
Final Concords of the county of Lincoln 1244-1272 ed C. W. Foster LRS 17 1920
Final Concords of Lincolnshire vol I pt I ed W. O. Massingberd London 1896
Letters and Papers, foreign and domestic, of the reign of Henry VIII preserved in the Public Record Office, the British Museum and elsewhere in England 23 vols in 38 London 1862-1932
Liber Feodorum, the Book of Fees, commonly called the Testa de Nevill 2 vols London 1920-1923
Lincoln Episcopal Records 1571-1584 ed C. W. Foster LRS 2 1912
Lincoln Wills 1271-1532 3 vols ed C. W. Foster LRS 5, 10, 24, 1914-1930
Lincolnshire Domesday and the Lindsey Survey eds. C. W. Foster and T. Longley LRS 19 1924

Lincolnshire Wills 1500-1600 ed A. R. Maddison Lincoln 1888

Pipe Roll Society Publications London 1884- (in progress)

Placitorum in Domo Capitulari Westmonsteriensi: asservatorum abbreviatio Record Commissioners London 1811

Placita de Quo Warranto Temp Ed I, II, III Record Commissioners London 1818

Port Books of Boston 1601-1640 ed R. W. K. Hinton LRS 50 1956

Prerogative Court of Canterbury Wills 1383-1558 British Record Society 10 and 11 1893-1895

Records of the Commissioners of Sewers in parts of Holland 1547-1608 2 vols eds A. M. Kirkus and A. E. B. Owen LRS 54, 63 1959-1968

Register of Bishop Philip Repingdon 1405-1419 2 vols ed M. Archer LRS 57, 58 1963

Register of Edward the Black Prince preserved in the Public Record Office 4 vols London 1930-1933

Registrum Antiquissimum of the Cathedral Church of Lincoln eds C. W. Foster and K. Major LRS 28, 32, 34, 41, 46, 51, 62 1933-1968

Rolls and Register of Bishop Oliver Sutton 1280-1299 ed R. M. T. Hill LRS 39, 43, 48, 52, 60, 64, 69 1948- (in progress)

Rotuli Hugonis de Welles 1209-1235 ed W. P. Phillimore, F. N. Davis et al RS 3, 6, 9 1919-1924

Rotuli Hundredorum temp Hen III et Ed I Record Commissioners London 1812

Rotuli de Liberate ac de misis et praestitis Reg John Record Commissioners London 1844

Rotuli Litterarum Clausarum Record Commissioners London 1833

Rotuli de Oblatis et Finibus Record Commissioners London 1835

Rotuli Parliamentorum 6 vols London 1832

Rotulorum Originalium in curia scaccarii abbreviatio Record Commissioners London 1805

Selden Society Publications 1885- (in progress)

Some Sessions of the Peace in Lincolnshire 1381-1396 ed E. G. Kimball LRS 49, 56 1955-1962

Syllabus of Rymer's Foedera 1066-1654 ed T. D. Hardy 2 vols London 1869-1873

Taxatio Ecclesiastica Angliae et Walliae auctoritate P. Nicholai IV, circa A.D.1291 Record Commissioners London 1802

Transcripts of Charters relating to the Gilbertine Houses ed F. M. Stenton LRS 18 1922

Valor Ecclesiasticus 6 vols Record Commissioners London 1825

Secondary Sources:

Allen, J. *A History of the County of Lincoln* vol 1 Lincoln 1834

Ballard, A. 'The English boroughs in the reign of John' *E.H.R.* 14 (1899) 93-104

Barbour, V. 'Dutch and English merchant shipping in the seventeenth century' *Ec.H.R.* I ser 2 (1929) 261-290

Barley, M. W. 'Lincolnshire rivers in the middle ages' *LAASRP* NS 1-2 (1936-37) 1-21

Barley, M. W. 'The Lincolnshire village and its buildings' *Linc Hist* 1 (1947-53) 252-272

Barley M. W. *The English Farmhouse and Cottage* London 1961

Barley M. W. *The House and Home* A visual history of modern Britain London 1963

Barley M. W. *Lincolnshire and the Fens* Yorkshire 1972

Barley M. W. *A Guide to British Topographical Collections* CBA Pub 1974

Barley M. W. (ed) *The plans and topography of medieval towns in England and Wales* CBA Research Report 14 1975

Bartlett J. N. 'The expansion and decline of York in the later middle ages' *Ec.H.R.* 2 ser 12 (1959) 17-33

Bean J. M. W. 'Plague, population and economic decline in England in the later middle ages' *Ec.H.R.* 2 ser 15 (1962) 423-437

Bedfordshire Historic Buildings: the heritage and its problems today Bedfordshire Historical Environment 1 (1975) Bedfordshire County Council Planning Department

Beresford M. W. *Lay subsidies and poll taxes* Phillimore 1963

Beresford M. W. *New towns in the middle ages* London 1967

Boston Archaeological Group Report 1961-1962 Boston 1962

Boston and South Lincolnshire Archaeological Group Report 1965-1966 Boston 1966

Bridbury A. R. *Economic growth: England in the later middle ages* London 1975

Buckatzsch E. J. 'The geographical distribution of wealth in England 1086-1843, *EcH.R.* 2 ser 3 (1950) 180-202

Carus-Wilson E. M. 'An industrial revolution of the thirteenth century' *Ec.H.R.* 1 ser 11 (1941) 39-60

Carus-Wilson E. M. 'Trends in the export of English woollens in the fourteenth century' *Ec.H.R.* 2 ser 3 (1950) 162-179

Carus-Wilson E. M. 'The medieval trade of the ports of the Wash' *Med Arch* vi-vii (1962-63) 182-201

Carus-Wilson E. M. and Coleman O. *England's Export Trade* 1275-1547 Oxford 1963

Clarke H. (ed) *Charters granted to the mayor and burgesses of the Borough of Boston* Stamford 1825

Cook A. M. *Boston: St. Botolph's town* Boston 1948

Darby H. C. *The medieval Fenland* Cambridge 1940

Darby H. C. *The Domesday geography of eastern England* Cambridge 1952

Davis G. R. C. *Medieval Cartularies of Great Britain* London 1958

Day L. J. C. 'The early monastic contribution to medieval farming' *Linc Hist* 1 (1947-53) 200-214

Dover P. *The early medieval history of Boston* 1086-1400 History of Boston Series 2 Kay Books 1972.

Down A. *Rescue Archaeology in Chichester* Phillimore 1974

Dugdale W. *The history of imbanking and drayning of rivers, fens and marshes* London 1662

Dugdale W. *Baronage of England* London 1676

Dugdale, W. *Monasticon Anglicanum* Bandinel B., Caley J. and Ellis H. (eds) 8 vols London 1817

East Midlands Archaeological Bulletins

Fowler Major G. 'Old river beds in the Fenland' *Geog J* 79 (1932) 210-213

Fowler Major G. 'Extinct waterways of the fens' *Geog J* 82 (1934) 30-36

Fuller G. J. 'Geographical aspects of the development of Boston 1700-1900' *East Mid Geog* 1, 2 (1954) 3-13

Gale J. *Registrum Honoris de Richmond* London 1772

Gillett E. *A History of Grimsby* Oxford 1970

Glassock R. E. 'The lay subsidy of 1334 for Lincolnshire' *LAASRP* NS1 0 (1964) 115-133

Gooder E. A. *Latin for local history: an introduction* Longmans 1961

Gould J. D. 'The inquisition of depopulation of 1607 in Lincolnshire' *E.H.R.* 67 (1952) 392-396

Grieve H. E. P. *Examples of English handwriting* 1150-1750 Essex Record Office Publications 1966

Gross C. *The Guild Merchant* 2 vols Oxford 1850

Hallam H. E. *Settlement and Society: a study of the early agrarian history of south Lincolnshire* Cambridge 1965

Haslam J. *Wiltshire Towns: the archaeological potential* Wiltshire Archaeological and Natural History Society 1976

Haward W. I. 'The trade of Boston in the fifteenth century' *LAASRP OS* 41-42 (1933-34) 169-178

Haley R. H. 'Medieval salt-making' *South Lincolnshire Archaeology* 1 (1977) 4-5

Hill J. F. W. *Medieval Lincoln* Cambridge 1948

Hinnebusch W. A. *The early English Friars Preachers* Rome 1952

Hinton R. W. K. 'Dutch entrepôt trade at Boston, Lincs., 1600-1640' *Ec.H.R.* 2 ser 9 (1956) 467-471

Hipkin G. M. 'Social and economic conditions in the Holland division of Lincolnshire 1640-1660' *LAASRP* OS 40 (1932) 137-256

Hodgett G. A. J. 'The Dissolution of the religious houses in Lincolnshire and the changing structure of society' *LAASRP* NS 4 (1952) 83-99

Hodgett G. A. J. *Tudor Lincolnshire* History of Lincolnshire VI Lincoln 1975

James M. K. 'Fluctuations in the Anglo-Gascon wine trade during the fourteenth century' *Ec.H.R.* 2 ser 4 (1951) 170-196

James M. K. *Studies in the medieval wine trade* Oxford 1971

Jebb G. *The church of St Botolph, Boston* Boston 1895

Jones S. R. *Four Minster Houses* Aberdeen 1974

Kershaw I. *Bolton Priory: the economy of a northern monastery* 1286-1325 Oxford 1973

Knowles D. and Neville-Hadock R. *Medieval religious houses of England and Wales* Longman 1971

Lambert M. R. and Walker R. *Boston, Tattershall and Croyland* Oxford 1930

Lappenberg J. M. *Urkundliche geschichte des Hansischen Stahlofer zu London* Hamburg 1851

Latham R. E. *Revised medieval Latin word list* Oxford 1965

Leech R. *Small medieval towns in Avon: archaeology and planning* Committee for Rescue Archaeology in Avon, Goucestershire and Somerset Survey No. 1 1975

Lees B. A. *Records of the Templars of England in the twelfth century* British Academy Records of Social and Economic History IX 1935

Lewis M. J. T. and Wright N. R. *Boston as a port* Proceedings of the seventh East Midlands Industrial Archaeology Conference Lincolnshire Industrial Archaeology Group 1973

Lincolnshire History and Archaeology Journals Archaeological Notes

May J. *Prehistoric Lincolnshire* History of Lincolnshire I Lincoln 1976

Mayes P. 'The medieval tile kiln at Boston, Lincs.' *J Arch Assoc* 3 ser 28 (1965) 86-109

Miller E. 'The fortunes of the English textile industry during the thirteenth century' *Ec.H.R.* 2 ser 18 (1965) 64-82

Miller S. H. and Skertchley S. J. P. *The Fenland past and present* London 1878

Molyneux F. H. and Wright N. R. *An atlas of Boston* History of Boston Series 10 Kay Books 1974

Moorhouse S. 'Finds from the excavations in the refectory at the Dominican Friary, Boston' *LHA* 7 (1972) 21-53

Morton W. K. *The history of St Botolph's church, Boston, Lincs.* Boston 1895

Musty A. E. S. *Excavations at Boston, Lincs. in 1972*

Myers A. R. *England in the late middle ages* Pelican History of England 4 Penguin Books 1971

Neilson N. *A terrier of Fleet, Lincs.* British Academy Records of Social and Economic History IV 1920

Owen D. M. *Church and Society in medieval Lincolnshire* History of Lincolnshire V Lincoln 1971

Pantin W. A. 'The merchants houses and warehouses of King's Lynn' *Med Arch* vi-vii (1962-63) 173-181

Parker V. *The making of King's Lynn* Chichester and London 1971

Pevsner N. and Harris J. *Lincolnshire* Penguin Books 1964

Phillips C. W. (ed) *The Fenland in Roman Times* Royal Geographic Society Research Series No 5 London 1970

Platt C. *Medieval Southampton: the port and trading community* 1000-1600 London 1973

Platt C. and Coleman-Smith R. (eds) *Excavations in medieval Southampton* 1953-1969 2 vols Leicester 1975

Platt C. *The English medieval town* London 1976

Porter H. *Boston* 1800-1868 typescript in Boston Library 3 vols 1941-1943

Postan M. M. *The medieval economy and society* Penguin Books 1972

Richardson H. G. 'Early history of the Commission of Sewers' *E.H.R.* 34 (1919) 385-393

Rodwell K. (ed) *Historic Towns in Oxfordshire: a survey of the new county* Oxfordshire Archaeological Unit Survey 3 Oxford 1975

Rodwell W. 'Hadstock' *Current Archaeology* IV 12 (1975) 375-381

Rogers A. *The medieval buildings of Stamford* Stamford Survey Group Report I Nottingham 1970

Rycraft A. *Sixteenth and seventeenth century handwriting I and II* University of York Borthwick Institute of Historical Research 1972

Rycraft A. *English medieval handwriting* and *Sixteenth and seventeenth century wills, inventories and other probate documents* University of York Borthwick Institute of Historical Research 1973

Sawyer P. H. (ed) *Medieval Settlement: continuity and change* Arnold 1976

Schofield R. S. 'The geographical distribution of wealth in England 1334-1649' *Ec.H.R.* 2 ser 18 (1965) 483-510

Simmons B. B. 'Ancient coastlines around the Wash' *South Lincolnshire Archaeology* I (1977) 6-9

Smith G. I. 'The land of Boston' *Land Use Survey Report* Part 69 London 1937

Stenton D. M. *English Society in the early middle ages* Pelican History of England 3 Penguin Books 1965

Stukeley W. *Itenarium Curiosum* London 1724

Swinnerton H. H. 'Post-glacial deposits of the Lincolnshire coast' *J Geol Soc* 87 (1931) 360-375

Swinnerton H. H. and Kent P. E. *The Geology of Lincolnshire* Lincolnshire Natural History Brochure 7 Lincolnshire Naturalist's Union Lincoln 1976

Thompson P. 'On the early commerce of Boston' *LAASRP OS* 2 (1853) 362-381

Thompson P. *History of Boston* 1856

Turner H. L. *Town defences in England and Wales* London 1971

Van Werveke H. 'Industrial growth in the middle ages: the cloth industry in Flanders' *Ec.H.R.* 2 ser 6 (1954) 237-245

Victoria County History of the County of Lincoln ed W. Page vol ii London 1906

Wells P. K. 'The excavation of a nineteenth century clay tobacco pipe kiln, Boston, Lincs.' *LHA* 5 (1970) 22-27

Wheeler W. H. *A history of the fens of south Lincolnshire* Boston 1896

Whitwell J. B. *Roman Lincolnshire* History of Lincolnshire II Lincoln 1970

Williamson D. M. 'Local documentary sources for a history of houses' *Linc Hist* I (1947-53) 303-306

Wood M. E. 'Measuring a medieval house' *Linc Hist* I (1947-53) 273-277